Endorsements

"THE GOLD IN FATHERING", is perhaps the most relatable, practical and intelligible guide you will find concerning the art and wisdom of fatherhood. Chris manages to masterfully and relevantly narrate both the personal, societal and spiritual significance of fatherhood in Uganda and globally. This book is convicting and uplifting at the same time. It is a MUST read!

Michael Badriaki, Executive Director at

Global Leadership Community, Washington State, USA

"Parenting – Mothering – Fathering: there are countless books about these subjects from religious, philosophical, political, and social perspectives, or a mix thereof. So what makes "The Gold in Fathering" special? I was taken by the style Chris has used, a mixture of experiential anecdotes and Bible verses, and the way he applies to both a forthright and frank style of reflection and narration that comes straight from his heart. Like any good book, this is a rich ore, and the reader must question, refine, and reflect on the contents. I have done that and I guarantee you one thing: the book is loaded with a lot of rich nuggets that will enrich my and your fathering experience. It is never too late to change for the better."

F. F. "Tusu" Tusubira,

Retired Professor, Rotary Leader and Consultant

I have watched and worked closely with Chris for the last ten years. I have seen him become a husband and a father, and not many are better qualified to address this extremely important and pressing issue; FATHERING! In The Gold In Fathering, Chris uses stories from his own life and family, weaving them together with powerful fathering principles that will help any reader become a better father. I highly recommend this book.

Moses Mukisa, Senior Pastor, Worship Harvest Church & Author; 'Called to Greatness'

This Book! It is a Rollercoaster of emotions; you laugh, cry, get enlightened, make mental notes and pray. I'm looking forward to purchasing copies for my papa, husband and papa-in-law. It is clearly very helpful for guys but it is also relevant for anyone who has/had a dad.

Roxanna Aliba Kazibwe, Author; 'My Love is not afraid'

Many of the most important things in life are caught and not taught. Nowhere is this more important than with fathers and their children. We have to be there to father them. In a world where every other sitcom is belittling, ridiculing and poking fun at the fathers and their roles in families it's refreshing to have a book that takes a wise, Biblical, logical and sometimes humorous look at a subject that just isn't dealt with enough. As a father of two adult children and two teenagers I can't help but wish I had had access to a book like this as I undertook my own journey to discover the Gold in Fathering.

Ransom Mahaka, NTV MEN Panelist

The prototype for fathering on the African continent generally looks like the character Okonkwo in the acclaimed Chinua Achebe book, "Things fall apart". Angry, aloof, detached, disinterested, volatile. This is not the case for every African man, but it certainly describes the relationship that most Africans have with their fathers. It is against this backdrop that "The Gold In Fathering" book by Chris Nsubuga-Mugga is written and in it he makes a compelling case for a different model of fathering that is based in the best examples of men that have fathered him over the years. This book is refreshing, candid, analytical and yet somehow manages to be a page turner. I would recommend it to any man that wants a better fathering prototype. I thoroughly enjoyed it and WILL be a better father for having read it!

Paulo Mugarura , Pastor Pivot 613, Ottawa, Ontario, Canada

My brother Chris D. Nsubuga-Mugga has written a stellar and timely book. A book for all to read but one that speaks specially to men and fathers. Using statistics, personal stories, "testimonies from the field", unforgettable quotations and biblical references, Chris challenges the reader to confront what Jim Collins in his book "Good to Great" refers to as the "brutal facts" – that fatherhood is the missing link in addressing many of the societal, leadership and governance questions of today. I can safely say that reading Chris' book makes me realize that we cannot discount the effect that fathering has on how we all turn out in life.

What makes this book very convincing to read is that Chris does not shy away from sharing his life's story with us. He reveals disappointments, mistakes (some quite embarrassing), celebrations and passion to us in a way that makes us understand that we are all human and that Fatherhood can be done right regardless of our background and experiences.

His final call to Father generations is a "wow" moment for me. A challenge to look beyond the four corners of my household - to reach out and father others (I call this mentorship) in more than one sphere of influence. This model can be replicated beyond our boundaries and lifetime- for posterity. In essence I glean from Chris' book that Fatherhood gives the highest results yet it is most ignored.

Now where is Daniel Jr my son? He and I need to "talk"

Daniel Ruhweza (PhD), Attorney and Lecturer at Law,
School of Law Makerere University

"The impact a father has on anyone's life is profound. Our world depends on every man choosing to be a great and loving father. It's a choice. In this book, Chris offers a blueprint for you to enjoy being the best father you can be. You will learn from the great fathers he has had, the great fathers around you and you will find success in mentoring those that call you father."

Julius Lukwago, CEO Solutions Africa

As I finished reading this book, all I could say was 'Wow'! This is truly an amazing book. Chris is an amazing story teller and weaver of truths and insights in a simple yet impactful way! I have always known about Chris' desire to be not just a good father, but a great father. I know he treasured the fathering he received from my father (whom I was totally glad to share with the many 'siblings' that came through our door). I am glad to say that I have seen Chris fulfill his desire of fathering his children with purpose and meaning. I have watched Chris father people at Worship Harvest, and now, in his role as pastor – he is a father over a young, but budding congregation in one of the Worship Harvest locations in Gayaza. Chris' heart lives and breathes fathering. But most of all, this heart for fathering comes from his long and deep relationship with the Father of us All - God the Almighty. I highly recommend this book. There are so many gold nuggets hidden in these pages. Buy the book for your dad, for your uncles, your brothers, your sons and for all your male friends!

The infusion of personal experiences and spirituality in explicating fathering, offers a groundbreaking philosophical text that fathers and readers alike will find incisive, palatable and instructive.

If you want to see a father at his best, watch Chris D. Nsubuga-Mugga. More than likely, you will initially feel that he's overdoing this father thing, especially if you are a father too. I mean, what's in fathering, we often think? Chris brings it all out. Chris is an intense guy, no doubt. He does his things to the maximum and that includes loving, mentoring and fellowshipping with his children. He is naturally a man of many words, so you can be sure that his kids hear the whole story! He's also great fun, so you know that the kids are going to get the best of it.

As much as a great book on fathering, The Gold in Fathering is a book about Chris' life. It's candid about the good, the bad and the ugly. It's also real fun to read! I could literally see Chris doing those pranks and not minding getting in trouble!

Chris, thank you for opening your heart and knowledge to us. I especially recommend this book to young fathers and those who are expecting to become fathers soon. The lessons in the book will prove invaluable.

In your hand is a book with practical, cross-cultural fathering tips. They are challenging and empowering; taking the reader from a worrying situation to one of hope. If you want to build a Godly heritage and legacy for your family, here are the 'How Tos' outlined by Chris D. Nsubuga-Mugga in "The Gold In Fathering".

I didn't have to read too far to identify myself with 'The Gold in Fathering.'

As a matter of fact, one could easily edit out Mr. Nsubuga's details and substitute them with mine. By seven years of age, I noticed that we had an absentee father, a heavy alcoholic, who always returned home in the wee hours to make every night a nightmare for the family. Mummy eventually called it quits, going away to start life on her own as a tailor. One by one, she picked us – two boys and three girls - from our father's house never to hear from him again. I can thus confess that I didn't experience anything like a father's love in the natural sense, which, in a way did affect me negatively as I grew into adulthood. Luckily, God brought several men into my life during the difficult years of adolescence, men who helped me to appreciate the concept of 'spiritual fatherhood.' I am indebted to these men of God for giving me that crucial foundation. Following their example, I made a conscious decision to be more intentional about becoming a father too. Thankfully, over the years, several fatherless young people – not my biological children - have gone through my hands – some under my personal care - to responsible adulthood. I am eternally thankful to them too for helping me to experience the joy of genuinely being called 'Daddy.' I rejoice to see the emotional stability, fervor, assertiveness, focus and vigour that my involvement brought into their lives. My desire is to be a father to many more children all over the world. I entirely agree with Chris that indeed there's 'gold in fathering.' I hope and pray that this long-overdue book will be used by God to unleash a new army of spiritual fathers for this our 'unfathered generation.'

Peter Nyanzi, Business Editor,
The Independent News Magazine

The Gold

In Fathering

UNLOCKING
THE FATHERING SECRETS
OF NOTABLE MEN

CHRIS D. NSUBUGA-MUGGA

Dedication

I dedicate this book to fathers; the men who have to figure out this challenging role and bear the weight of this great responsibility on a daily basis in all the families around the world. I honor you. I celebrate your achievements. I encourage you not to give up. I believe in your dreams. Your labor is not in vain.

I specifically dedicate this book to all the men that fathered me; Henry B. Mugga Basazzemagya, Rev. Canon Benoni Mugarura (Uncle Ben), Pastor Chris Komagum, Apostle John Bunjo, Ernest Ssentongo Kibalama (RIP), Steven Karebi (RIP), Sam Mutono and Joseph Kaddu. I am a result of your collective effort.

Lastly, to the only woman befitting this honor role - Rachel Ntongo (my MAFAZA). It has been a long road and I am glad you never gave up on me despite the challenge I was.

Contents

Acknowledgements

My wife, Lynnet K. Nsubuga – you are God's wonderful treasure to me. You are a loyal and faithful friend. You are a great conversationalist and a very wise woman. The brilliance of your mind still has me in awe. You have made the later part of my life a lot more meaningful than the lost and lonely years. Thank you for the numerous hours that you have allowed me to curve out of our time in order to write and publish this book. I like you very much.

Lemuel and Sinza my children, you have made fathering a pleasant experience. I love you to bits. You are God's gifts to me. Your encouragement on this book writing journey has been amazing.

I want to thank my Parents for all your love and counsel. Dad, I have enjoyed the conversations we have in Ntinda. Mum (Ntinda), thank you for treating me honorably since I first met you. Rachel Ntongo my mother, you are an amazing pillar of strength, courage and love. Thank you for introducing me to the most important relationship in my life – one with God.

My siblings Ronnie, Mabel, Rebecca, Juliana, Olga and Jennifer, I love the way we are gelling these days. Our 'Bako' Fabian, Chris and Daniel, thank you for treating our sisters well. You are honorable men. The amazing and industrious Lydia Mugga, thanks for keeping my big bro on the path of true success.

Paulo Ayebare Mugarura – you are more than a best friend, you are my brother. Introducing me to your family; the Mugarura family was the best thing that ever happened to me. Uncle Ben, Aunt Joy, Jackie, Gloria, Rachel and Peter (Twonjex), thank you for your love and acceptance. Thank you for sharing the most impactful man in my life with me.

Steven and Michelle Shalita, you are the best gift of friendship there ever will be. Your example of parenting is a script that Lynnet and I read from. Thank you for opening up your lives to us.

Worship Harvest Church, you are my home away from home. I agree with the writer who said, better a friend nearby than a brother far off. You indeed are my family. The Worship Harvest Gayaza family, you all rock!!! Life without you would have been incomplete. The elders at Worship Harvest, you are the real deal!!! The Agabas, Kattos, Rutabingwas and Kiryowas, your pouring into my life will never be forgotten. The Mukisas, Byemanzis, Baalesanvus, Makhandes, Kisas, Okullos, Kawesas, Rusokes,

Beresis, Kwatamporas and Mukasas; you have shared with me your Time, Treasure and Talent; withholding nothing!!! Thank you. We have a big vision and I am looking forward to the ride.

The church families of St. Francis Chapel (Makerere), St Andrews C.O.U Bukoto and Watoto, my story can never be complete without you. Thank you. Rev. Moses Isabirye, your fathering heart has extended a warm hand of fellowship to us and to many. Pastors Gary and Marilyn Skinner, I learnt leadership at a distance from you. Thank you for being real.

Paul Kisakye, my editor, thank you for your tireless work and advice. To the most encouraging critical readers, Roxanna Aliba Kazibwe and Angela Sanyu Okullo, thank you for your time and advice.

The Nomad creative team led by Jeremy Byemanzi, you make everything you touch look good.

I am grateful to General Katumba Wamala for writing the foreword of this book. Your example of Fathering – humility, discipline and encouragement defines who you are no matter what office you hold. I have quietly admired both your public and private life. Thank you for looking out for disadvantaged children. Thank you for fathering through Rahab Uganda and so many other ventures. You are truly a father worth celebrating.

I would like to thank the Kawesas (Uncle Voomvoom & Aunt Ritah), the Segwayas. ARK and the Ssentongos (Sese). Some friendships are short lived, others are for a life time. Thank you for true friendship.

Lastly and most importantly, I would like to thank God for bringing me this far; my life means nothing without You Lord. You have been my Father from the very beginning and I continue to enjoy Your love. Thank you.

Foreword

I have always found it interesting and a tad bit peculiar how, in many cultures, deliberate efforts are taken to train girls, right from childhood to be good mothers. They are taught how to cook for the family, bathe the babies and how to nurture respect for their future husbands. On the other hand, however, I've found it disturbing how (in my view) not so much deliberate effort is made to empower the boys in becoming fathers. They are taught to work and fend for a family alright, but to father? No. In other aspects, there is a tendency of men divorcing their parenting responsibilities to mums, house maids and gargets like TVs, and Computers in the name of working hard.

Quite often, spending time with their children; loving them, correcting them and modeling a life worth following, is something most fathers have had to learn on the job. Chris D. Nsubuga-Mugga has taken up the mantle to help men become better fathers. He speaks pointedly and non-judgmentally perhaps because he understands both the pain of being fatherless and the 'how-to-father' struggle as a father of two. His book is a sincere account of a father not from hearsay or how I saw it but from real experience of how he has done it.

When Chris asked me to read his book 'THE GOLD IN FATHERING', I accepted without hesitation. I wanted to hear what he had to say on the subject. By the time I got to the middle of the book, I believed him. The passion and genuineness with which he writes jump off the pages and draw you in. The book has relatable anecdotes at the beginning of every chapter that causes you to reflect on your own life. Chris seasons each call to action with hope and encouragement.

When I first met Chris, he was the guest speaker on Father's day (Sunday 15th June, 2014) at St. Andrew's Church – Bukoto. As he had done the previous year, he fired up most of the men in Father's Union with his encouragement and challenge. He spoke with the same palpable passion that one captures in this book. I enjoyed this writ a lot more than I had anticipated. It is a very relevant book for Men and fathers all over the world.

Having survived through many potentially fatal experiences, Chris believes that he has lived this long, to write this book. I can assert that if you have had 'Daddy Issues' the situation would have been different had you or your father read this book beforehand. Chris exhorts us. He shows that it is not too late for reconciliation and restoration. Being a great father can be learned. It is in every man's DNA. It is willed by God. It just needs to be activated.

What you hold in your hand is the activation key for great fathering experiences.

Do not expect any judgment about your past mistakes from this book. Do not expect someone to lord it over you concerning what you have to do or not do. Expect genuine practical help on fathering with a scriptural and experiential backing from fathering stories of many notable men.

I recommend this book for all men, for fathers and for everyone who has a father/father figure. Its worthy for real mothers too – those with whom fathers share the role of parenting. We all need this book.

Whatever point you are at in your life, it is not too late to lay hold of THE GOLD IN FATHERING.

Gen. Katumba Wamala Edward
Chief of Defense Forces (CDF),
Uganda People's Defense Force (UPDF)

Introduction

When I was seven years old, my father was not home for a long while. It was in this season that my mother started religiously attending services at Makerere Redeemed of the Lord Evangelistic Church. In those days, the Sunday services in these kinds of churches took eons. A typical service was usually more than four hours. For seven-year-old me, the three kilometer walk back home from church was always near torture. By the time we arrived, I would be totally famished.

The newly-found brotherly love from this church, however, did not go down well with my brother Ronnie and I. There was a certain man, whose face had a depression on the forehead. For some reason, my mother called him 'Brother'. He warmly welcomed us into the church and took it upon himself to walk us home every Sunday. He made it a habit to see to it that we were settled in before he left. Gentlemanly as that might look, we were bothered that he too always settled himself in and engaged our mother and us in what seemed to be mindless small talk even for a boy my age.

We always had Pillau, an Indian dish of well-spiced rice and beef, on Sundays. It was the only day we could have it because of our economic means. We soon discovered that this new 'Brother' had more ideas for our Pillau than he did for our safety and comfort. He always stayed long enough to gorge lots of Pillau and would summarily depart thereafter. This bothered Ronnie and I a lot. We started actively pursuing a solution.

I was never short on mischief so one Sunday afternoon; I seized an opportunity to settle our score with this 'Brother'. After going through the motions, just when the whiff of almost-ready Pillau made it into our little sitting room, this 'Brother' stood up. When he turned around, noticed that his trousers had a hole in their behind. I used my index finger to repeatedly poke at him through the hole as I gleefully declared that the 'Brother' had a hole in his trousers.

The poor man was too embarrassed to stay for the meal that day. We did not see him again thereafter and you can be certain that we did not miss him.

Had my father been around, I don't think I would have been able to pull such a prank on that man. This was not the first time I had lived apart from my father. It certainly was not to be the last.

There is a crisis of fatherlessness in a number of countries today. The statistics do not paint a beautiful picture. More than one third of American children live in a home without the physical presence of a father. An estimated 24.7 million children (33%) in the United States of America (USA) live absent from their biological father[1]. Millions more have dads who are physically present, but emotionally absent. If it were classified as a disease, fatherlessness would be an epidemic worthy of attention as a national emergency[2]. According to 72.2% of the U.S. population, fatherlessness is the most significant family or social problem facing America[3].

The situation in Jamaica is much worse. Their 2011 census shows that over 80% of Jamaican children were born out of wedlock. The majority of these did not even have their father's name – the most basic association with a father – on their birth certificate[4].

All over the world, there is an increase in female-headed households; Benin (22.9%), Cameroon (25.5%), Uganda (29.5%), Comoros (39.3%), Dominican Republic (39.9%), Haiti (40.6%)[5] The data on fatherlessness in these countries is not as rich as it is in the US but one gets a sense that countries like Uganda are not too far behind the US and if the situation goes unchecked, they shall soon be playing in the fatherlessness big league with Jamaica.

Some fathering advocates would say that almost every social ill faced by children is related to fatherlessness. Children from fatherless homes are more likely to be poor, become involved in drug and alcohol abuse, drop out of school, and suffer from health and emotional problems. Boys are more likely to become involved in crime, and girls are more likely to become pregnant as teens[6].

The commonly asked question is, "Where are the fathers?"

Now, much as I think this to be a well intended question, it sounds every bit condescending and creeks with undertones that are out of touch with the plight of many men across the globe.

Most men desire to be great fathers. They desire to enjoy all the benefits that accrue from being a great father: stable families, prosperity and success for their children, an admirable legacy and posterity. These fathers desire that their children walk on ground more sure footed than the one on which they've walked. This, my friend, is the Gold in Fathering and many men seek to lay hold of it.

William Shakespeare said, "It is a wise father that knows his own child."

Many fathers totally agree with him yet many questions still linger in their minds. Why is the fathering situation we desire so far from the one we experience? Do we have the right fathering model? Is any man actually taught how to be a father? Can I teach my sons to be better fathers than our generation?

Many men desire to be better fathers than they are and, in many cases, better fathers than their fathers. They just don't know how to.

In this book, I seek to point you to the source of fathering, what fathering truly is and how we can father nations and generations into the future.

Like all true treasure, the Gold in Fathering has secret truths which, when embraced, can make a great father of any man on the face of the earth. The pages that follow in this book will unlock these fathering secrets to you. My hope and prayer is that this book will change the course of your life and the fortunes of your sons and daughters for the better.

Chapter One: Fathering from Birth

Rachel Ntongo, lying on a bed at Nsambya hospital, looked on helplessly as the nurses cried out for help. She was only 23 years old and this could turn out for the worst. The curtains flung open and Dr. Miriam Duggan, the resident gynaecology and obstetrics doctor, swung into action. She expertly pulled away the umbilical cord that was certainly going to suffocate Rachel's infant at birth.

After a few reassurances and painful contractions, at 7:45am, on Sunday 24th October, 1976, she delivered a baby boy weighing 3.5 kilos. The baby let out a loud cry, to the joy of his mother and relief of the attending nurses, who had all this while held their breath, hoping for the best.

That baby was me.

A few moments of delay could have taken my life. Any slight hesitation could have denied me the opportunity to live, to be fathered and also father others.

From a very young age, life threw many curve balls my way but I somehow survived the numerous incidents that could have ended my life. I got chicken pox twice and almost died the second time.

As a toddler, I drank a quarter of a bottle of paraffin while my mother polished the floor. My eyes rolled. My mother rushed me to hospital just in time to save my life. I have had a car run over my foot thrice and survived being run over by a military armored vehicle by a whisker. I have survived 13 robberies and lived through three wars that could have taken my life.

My father, Henry Beckman Mugga Basazzemagya, is an insurer at heart and is good at accounts and property brokerage. He knows every nook and cranny of Kampala, the capital city of Uganda.

When I was born, my father was considered part of the middle class in Uganda at the time. He worked with Hog & Robinson, a leading insurance firm in the country. He owned two brand new fiat cars as was the mark of the middle class in 1976. He had returned from London two years prior and almost single handedly footed the bill of his wedding reception at Lugogo indoor stadium. He belonged to a different middle class from the one we see in Uganda today, where relatives and friends have to raise money and pitch in with contributions for any wedding to happen.

At the time I was born, my father had already experienced being a father when my brother Ronnie and my sister Mabel were born. I was another reminder of a role and responsibility that he already knew he carried. He was a father. Just like his father before him and the numerous generations of men that came before him, he had to carry the mantle of fatherhood.

In one sense he knew he was going to be a father again, yet in another sense, fatherhood had been thrust upon him just like it is for many men. In times past, men were barely told how critical the role of fathering was. They were never really told about the gigantic proportions of responsibility that they bore as fathers. I don't think it is any different now.

When a boy is born, the odds are that he will be a father someday. Apart from eunuchs, who we only read about, and faithful Roman Catholic priests, fatherhood almost feels inevitable. In fact the Roman Catholic priests do not escape it either, for they operate in a space where they are rightly called 'Father'.

Lucky Dube sang, 'Big boys don't cry'. The heart of this narrative is that a boy must toughen up in order to get ready for manhood and, consequently, for fatherhood. Even though it's a tell tale sign for what is coming ahead, unfortunately, that's mostly all you get to hear about fathering.

Chris Brown, a popular American recording artist, said, "What's on the surface always looks like one big party but inside there is a little boy looking for help and guidance. People say, 'Be a man'. Yeah, that's right but it doesn't take away any pain you really go through. I just wanna stay out the way and do music. Most importantly and (be a) great father. I don't have any more patience for anything that will cause me to self destruct!"[7]

While the girl child is accorded lots of counsel from her mother and her aunts about motherhood, the story is usually different for the boy child. You are usually meant to figure things out in the school of hard knocks. The training usually presumes that if you tinker with it long enough, you will figure it out.

Honestly, it is akin to getting a twelve year old village boy from the middle of nowhere and launching him in a rocket to the moon with a hope that when he gets there, he will figure things out.

That's the plight of most men around the world. No one really teaches us how to be fathers and yet society's conditioning says to us that asking about it really makes us look bad, weak and not men worth our salt. As a result, we pretend to know what we are doing, putting on a tough exterior, yet on the inside, we are crying out for help like a child.

On 1st December, 2005 at 5pm, my wife, Lynnet, made an announcement that most men would dread to hear at home.

The waters had broken and the baby was on the way.

I was home alone with her and did not have a moment to spare to ponder what I could or could not do. I bundled her into the car and drove as fast as I could.

I had attended every single antenatal visit she had gone for. We had even done extra preparation classes for the baby. But nothing ever really prepares you for these moments.

Adrenaline rushed through my blood. My heart raced. I had to get her to hospital before the baby got stressed. I had the disadvantage of knowing too much about the consequences of any delay. The classes and loads of prior reading had got me into a panic.

I sped past every moving thing I found on the road. Pedestrians, bicycles, cars, trucks, name it. I was determined to get my wife and baby to safety.

We arrived at International Hospital Kampala (IHK) at 6pm and had an emergency check in. I was glad that we had fully paid the delivery package; sometimes paying as little as fifty thousand Uganda shillings, then equivalent to 15 US dollars, per month. We were not necessarily people with means. We just wanted the best for our baby.

My wife was checked in and the midwives confirmed the baby's heart beat was normal. We sighed in relief.

As grateful smiles were beginning to brighten our faces, she winced in pain. Very strong contractions started. She was clearly in agony and I wished I could take some of the pain away. Of course that's what I felt like in that moment. I have however watched a YouTube video of two very brave men who experienced a simulation of birth contractions. The previously braggart fellows were crying like babies in a few moments[8].

Hats off to all our mothers!

The pressure of bringing forth a baby can only be experienced to understand it. I had really looked forward to having a child yet on the other hand, I did not want to lose my wife in labor. It was a combination of hope and fear, bravery and cowardice. It was like being at the battle front, where even the atheist prays to God when the bullets start flying and the bombs start landing.

We were taken into a private delivery room. After a while, a student nurse walked in with a file. She started reading all the hospital policies to my wife and wanted her to consent to each and every one of them in order to indemnify the hospital against any eventualities of her delivery.

I thought her to be one of the most heartless creatures on God's created earth. This was the worst time to read a list to my wife.

After a while, her barrage of tormenting questions, especially when my wife was having strong contractions, got to me. I told her that was enough. I demanded to sign the papers or she had to leave immediately.

We argued for a while until we reached a compromise.

By the time we had gotten rid of the student nurse, the contractions were coming quick and fast. We were having what doctors call a precipitated labor. My wife started using the bathroom a little too often. The baby was really close.

In one of those times, she got a contraction while seated on the pan and she came off with the toilet seat and cover!

The strength of women during contractions needs to be harnessed for baby delivery and moving heavy earth equipment all at the same time. It's amazing what a small woman can lift when she has a strong contraction.

Dr. Carol Ssekimpi, a friend of ours who worked at IHK, walked in just in time to assure us and bemusedly watch, as my wife manhandled me through the contractions. Fingers squeezed against my wedding ring. My shirt was roughed up. I was asked to sit and stand at the same time whenever a contraction came. I was however determined to be there when our first born came out of her womb.

An experienced midwife came in and issued commands to the attending nurses. Moments later, after things got more chaotic and the noise levels in the room had reached those of a busy downtown market, out came this tiny baby with whitish stuff all over his body. I was extremely glad that the moment I had waited for had come. He let out a baby cry and was placed on the chest of his mother.

I was given the scissors and I cut the umbilical cord.

Bang!

I was a father!

In what has now become poetic truth, I cut that umbilical cord: disjoined Lemuel from his mother, and from that point, my fathering responsibilities began. I did the same for Sinza, our daughter three years later. I cut their umbilical cords. I had started my tenure for life as their father and no matter what it took, I had to figure it out.

The weeks that followed the birth of both our children were interesting. The baby would seemingly sleep for a micro second and be awake the whole night. Sleep became a rare, precious commodity.

Helping out was not debatable, although the baby always seemed to be fixated on soiling every diaper as soon as it was changed. I have never gotten over how many diapers I bought during that time.

The next time you visit a couple that just had a baby, carry a pack of diapers. Do it for the guy. That's one of the most loving things you can do for him. He will love you to bits.

When you become a father, the excitement of all your work colleagues wears off quickly. You have to get back to work immediately, without missing a beat on your stellar performance.

Not many people understand why you are napping through meetings as you try to cover for your sleep debt. They don't understand when you skip going out to the high end restaurants for meals as you try to save in order to keep up with the diaper race that your little bundle of joy seems to be beating you at.

They also don't understand you checking out in a trance mid-conversation as you ponder what fatherhood is going to be like or the pressure that builds within. Pressure to provide. Pressure to protect. Pressure to be a good example to follow. Pressure!

Most of the pressure however is internally generated. Men are very competitive. That's who we are and, unfortunately, that builds lots of internal pressure when we compare ourselves with others.

Joseph Atukunda, a guest on NTV MEN, a leading TV magazine program on which I am a panelist, once said "Men set themselves a standard that is too high to attain". I could not agree more. Joseph had recovered from mental illness a few years before. He was sharing his struggles with us, which he thought led to the stress that he and others faced, leading them into depression and mental illness in some cases.

You see, the challenge that men face daily is that you have got to have your act together. You are usually in a leadership position and leaders must know where they are going. Your wife, your children, your workmates, your neighbors, your friends and society at large expect you to know what you are doing.

There is very little wiggling space and almost no room for error. Literally everything depends on you. At least that's what you are brought up to think.

So how dare you say that you have no clue about being a father? There is absolutely no way. The typical man sucks it in, bears the brunt for his mistakes and hopes to God that He will understand his plight or weaknesses on judgment day. Therefore, men usually only make do with knowing that they have done their best with the hand that life dealt them.

Many fathers cannot be able to tell another man how to be a good father. In Uganda, the phrase you hear the most from the men is, "I am trying."

Not improving. Not excelling. But trying.

In other parts of the world, this may be said differently but it is essentially the same notion you get from men you meet anywhere in the world.

I have had the privilege of speaking to numerous men about their lives. What stands out though is that about 8 out of 10 of the men that I have spoken with in Uganda have daddy issues. Absentee fathers, uninvolved fathers, abusive fathers, mean fathers, unresponsive fathers, resigned fathers and the list goes on.

Has your experience been any different?

What has led us as men to sink to such lows? How is it that the champions in the area of fathering are so few and far

between? Is there hope for men who want to be great fathers? Is the Gold in Fathering really attainable?

I believe it is.

In fact you are going to soon find out that as a man, you are wired for fatherhood! It's in your DNA and it can be learnt. It can be improved. Matter of fact, you can excel at it.

Chapter Two: Fathering from the Source

Paul Hunter, one of the best and most passionate fathers I know, once said, "God created the earth intending us to be one big family with a Father. The devil on the other hand has been trying to make us one big orphanage – Fatherless."

While fathering is hardwired within our system, it can also be learnt. God is the Father of all and since the fall of Adam, man has been removed from the best classroom environment on fatherhood: a relationship with God the Father.

Some of the Oxford English Dictionary definitions of father are:

A man, in relation to a child or children born from an ovum that he has fertilized.

An ancestor.

A man who founds something, first leads somebody/ something, or is the most important influence in the early history of something.

To become a parent of somebody.

To create or devise something.

Father is both a verb (an action) and a noun (name). God is our Father because He created us and Father is also His name – Father God or God the Father. I can't emphasize enough how important this truth is in helping us to be great fathers.

The sorry state of fatherhood can only point to the fact that a wrong model has been passed down to us. If the same mistake is repeated from one generation to another, it means that we have been reading from the same failed script all this time.

Albert Einstein once said, "Insanity is doing the same thing over and over again and expecting different results."

The information that the majority of fathers have had on fatherhood is wrong. The models of fatherhood are skewed or absent. It is not a pretty picture.

According to Mike Breen and Steve Cockram[10], we learn best through a combination of information, imitation and innovation. It's not enough for us to hear about what fathering is like, we need to see it up close and personal in order for us to relate with it and copy it. It is only after imitating fathering long enough that we can become masters at it and innovate better ways of doing it.

If you are really good at anything, you must have heard accurate information about it, been apprenticed by someone who is really good at it and also been given the space to practice it on your own. That's how doctors and architects are trained. They take five years of class work with some research and limited practical work. They then have to do two years of apprenticeship before they are given license to practice on their own authority.

Being a father is no different. I would argue that actually more time is needed to make great fathers. After all, balanced and successful human beings are of more value than buildings and cadavers.

From the very onset, you can see how every failed fatherhood is a by-product of satan's work.

Every time a man fails at the responsibilities that fatherhood brings, the trophy goes to the devil, not to God.

Here is why. Children grow up fatherless, abused and raped in some cases. Wives crave the affection of a loving man to no avail. Many times, estranged wives end up in the arms of more than one man with the label "Use and dump" stuck on their foreheads. The men themselves never really operate at their best knowing they walked out on their own children.

No man ever wants to fail as a father.

You were created (fathered) by God after His image. So no one should ever tell you that you cannot be a great father.

Then God said, "Let Us make man in Our image, according to Our likeness; let them have dominion over the fish of the sea, over the birds of the air, and over the cattle, over all the earth and over every creeping thing that creeps on the earth." So God created man in His own image; in the image of God He created him; male and female He created them. (Genesis 1:26-27)

You are the exact representation of your Maker, especially when you are restored to the original state by faith in Jesus Christ.

You have all it takes to hold the responsibilities of fatherhood excellently. You already have it in you. For many of us, we have only got to believe it and learn from the inside out.

Fathering is too important a role and fatherhood too important a responsibility for me to tip toe around it, in a bid to be politically correct. So allow me say some things as they really are.

Fathers are stewards of the children they are given whether they be biological or not. Children are a gift from God.

Behold, children are a heritage from the Lord, The fruit of the womb is a reward. (Psalm 127:3)

Fathering is a sacred trust. God has entrusted you with those precious ones. They may bear your name, look like you, talk like you and walk like you but they are His gift to you. You are a steward.

My wife and I have a property we are developing. We once hired a caretaker from whom we learnt a lot about stewardship.

He started off pretty well. He was a responsible and honest young man.

The place had been looking like a mess. When we hired him, we told him exactly what we desired the place to look like. We painted a really clear picture. In no time, the place looked like what we desired and we were glad.

He later on got into planting tomato and cabbage gardens for himself all over the village. He even started looking after pigs. Obviously, there was nothing wrong with him doing business. We encourage entrepreneurship wherever we find it.

However, we had a small problem. He no longer had our picture in mind. At some point it looked like our purpose for hiring him was the distraction. His tomatoes, cabbages and two pigs were his main preoccupation.

Once when we asked him to help the builders to collect some water for construction from a nearby well, he sulked and threw an adult tantrum for a full week! He forgot that he was a steward of our property and still needed to defer to us on how it was run.

We cannot be fathers (stewards of earthly fatherhood) and ignore the desire and design of God the Father.

If you fail to father your children right, God will find other men who will. He is determined that all children, all sons and daughters experience His love.

Will you be His conduit as an earthly father?

There is however a quagmire concerning fathering that must be resolved early on.

Have you ever been travelling in a car or bus and started a conversation on the phone, then got to a place with low connectivity and, just before you got to the reason why you called, the call got disconnected?

Therein lays our challenge. We are meant to father while connected to

God the Father. When there is no signal, the call is dropped and we are left to keep guessing what to do with these children we were given.

Jesus offers us a great example on fathering. Though He had no biological children, He being the first born of many in the family of God, is a surrogate father.

In John 13:33, Jesus refers to his followers as little children. He shows us that fatherly authority flows from God the Father. He also demonstrates a high level of commitment to fathering that can only be started, maintained and guaranteed through us by God the father only.

For I have come down from heaven, not to do My own will, but the will of Him who sent Me. This is the will of the Father who sent Me, that of all He has given Me I should lose nothing, but should raise it up at the last day. (John 6:38-39)

My sheep hear My voice, and I know them, and they follow Me. And I give them eternal life, and they shall never perish; neither shall anyone snatch them out of My hand. My Father, who has given them to Me, is greater than all; and no one is able to snatch them out of My Father's hand. (John 10:27-29)

Jesus uses a metaphor of sheep to mean children or followers (people someone influences and cares deeply about). If you recall the Oxford English dictionary definitions of father, this is still consistent with being a father.

Jesus says that God's will is not to lose any of those given to Him. Have you ever thought that God does not want you to ever lose any of your children as a father? Your children and the generations that will come from them are as precious as gold. No one trifles with gold.

Jesus even goes on to say that no one will snatch them out of His hands. God the Father will make sure that does not happen. No one is stronger than Him. He is the Father and is interested in you succeeding at fathering.

You have God on your side. He is cheering you on. He wants you to be a great father. He is there to guarantee that you do not lose any of the children that He has given you. If you are plugged in and connected to Him, that is a promise that you can take to the bank. You are not alone.

In verse 28, Jesus mentions giving eternal life to His sheep (followers or children). It is interesting to see what Jesus Himself defines eternal life to be:

And this is eternal life, that they may know You, the only true God, and Jesus Christ whom You have sent. (John 17:3)

Eternal life oozes out of knowing God the Father and Jesus the Son, who also acts as surrogate Father to us. The knowing here comes from fellowship, communion, communication and being one. This is akin to when a wife says of a husband she has been married to for 25 years, "I really know my husband."

I would like to suggest to you that there is amazing life that oozes from you as a father to your children when you spend time with them, play with them, talk with them and they know you.

On September 10th, 2015, Mugote Timothy, my friend, posted this on Facebook: "Today, I celebrate the man who grew me, Sam Mugote my old man, recently graduated to Kaka, Dada, Grandpa. He is the smartest guy on the planet and knows something about everything. (He) is a Linguist, an Engineer, Guitarist, Pianist, Bishop, Farmer, NGO director, CEO, Businessman, and best of all, a very principled mentor. He and I are like Best Buddies, his wisdom is shocking as is his strong headedness (guess the apple does not fall too far from the tree). Love you dad and may you continually grow more refined and may years never touch you. The grey in your hair is just but a sign of God's glory in you".

Be encouraged on your fathering journey. It is easier than we have been coached to believe. For us to do it right, we just have to be connected to the Father of Love and in the way that he ordained us to be connected to Him.

Did you know, that you have an inbuilt receiver that connects you to God?

You have a spirit.

But there is a spirit in man: and the inspiration of the Almighty giveth them understanding. (Job 32:8, KJV)

You are not just a heap of soil that somehow evolved into who you are today. You are not a piece of male flesh, making the numbers of the world's population, helping us reach seven billion living humans.

You are a spirit, you have a soul and live in a body. This is how God the Almighty inspires you and gives you understanding on fathering. God is spirit and essentially relates with you that way.

Another version of this same scripture says;

But there is a spirit in man, and the breath of the Almighty gives him understanding. (Job 32:8)

After His resurrection and before Jesus ascended into heaven, He breathed on His disciples. It is important to see what that leads to:

So Jesus said to them again, "Peace to you! As the Father has sent Me, I also send you." And when He had said this, He breathed on them, and said to them, "Receive the Holy Spirit. (John 20:21-22)

The breath of the Almighty is the reconnection that helps your spirit to be joined with His Holy Spirit. There is lots of wisdom and counsel that the Holy Spirit has given to men who have received Him for thousands of years before us. This flow of wisdom and counsel from the Holy Spirit is available to us now and will continue to be till the end of time. That counsel goes beyond fathering. It gets into business, investments, choice of spouse, career, securing a home for your family, etc.

The details of this reality are beyond the scope of this book. I just want to show you that you have a spirit, which is fully able to tap into God's inspiration, giving understanding on what to do as a father.

Recently, I was requested by the Principal of Harvest Academy, a leading international Christian curriculum school in Kampala, to speak to the young boys there about sex and sexuality. It was both an easy and challenging task. Easy, because I have no qualms talking to anyone about sex, since the day it dawned on me that sex is good, pleasurable and ordained by God for relationship and procreation in the confines of marriage.

Here was my challenge: one of the boys was my first born, nine-year-old son, Lemuel. I could not approach this task with shock and awe, dropping the bombs carelessly. Now, although I do not drop bombs carelessly, I had more pressure because it suddenly dawned on me that I am not just a facilitator of conversation on sex and sexuality. I am also Lemuel's father.

By God's grace, I finally figured out a way of speaking to my nine year old and his classmates in the most fatherly and candid of ways. It was challenging yet very fruitful.

God will always give you a spark of an idea, a thought or a concept. Our walk as fathers is not a lone walk. We walk with the Father of all.

One of the most amazing experiences for me during this talk was seeing Lemuel and the other little boys wide eyed about who they really are and the differences between them and the girls.

When it came to sex, one of the questions we discussed was whether they were ready to become fathers.

They were shocked, bewildered, confused and in denial all at the same time. Cartoons come closest to the picture I saw: eyes popping out, hair standing on end and all limbs stiff. For these little boys, their reaction was justified. They were not ready for fathering.

I have seen a similar or worse trepidation in the eyes of grown men concerning fathering, albeit quite disguised on the outside.

Why are we scared of fathering?

I can hear you push back, "Who said I am scared of being a father?" Well, hold your reins for a moment.

I am not talking about the under-three-minutes-act of pleasure. That, even dogs can have. So it's not the biology that I am talking about. It's the responsibilities.

It's the being woken up at night when the baby is crying, the changing of diapers when your wife is in the kitchen preparing you a meal, taking the children for the evening walk, telling them bed-time stories, paying their school fees, being imitated by them, including all the mannerisms you are not proud of, and leaving them an inheritance. That is scary!

When Lemuel was four years old, he developed a habit that I could not stand. He ended almost every word in every sentence with the exclamation, "Eeh!?"

What should have been, "Daddy, are you going to take me to school?" became "Daddy-eeh!? Are you eeh !?! going eeh!?! To take me-eeh!? To school-eeh!?"

What was he doing? Who told him that he could get away with such mindless repetitions in my house? I was furious at this little boy for such a long time. Then one day, as I spoke to my wife, it all came crashing in my face like a ton of bricks. I was the reason that Lemuel spoke like that. He only picked one "eeh!?" at the end of a phrase, multiplied it and applied it generously to every word he knew.

I did not know whether to laugh or cry. I was petrified and appalled that he could imitate me that much. I then wondered what else he had picked up. I was not concerned about the good stuff I do. I was most concerned about the stuff I am not so proud of.

Here is a question that I would like you to wrestle with for a while: Would you be glad if your son or daughter turned out to be exactly the way you are?

Score that on a scale of one to ten.

Your answer to that question is the score of where your fathering is. That is the state of your fatherhood.

I know that not many of us would score highly on this question if we were honest. I do hope that you will honestly score higher the next time you are faced with this question. I hope you will score higher after reading this book.

There is good news for all men. We can all grow into great fathers. It is possible to score 10 out of 10 on that question.

Chapter Three: Fathering is Love

He had lice crawling all over his body. He stunk to the high heavens and went many weeks without taking a bath. He ate left over dumped food that had been served and rejected by mentally retarded patients at Mulago Hospital. He lived in the slums of Katanga near Mulago, a suburb of Kampala.

He was a drunkard and a malnourished adult man with kwashiorkor. His belly was extended and his feet were swollen. There was nothing that anyone desired in this notorious drunk called Benoni Mugarura Mutana. To cap all that, he had dropped out of school in Senior three (the equivalent of grade 10).

This dirty, stinking, uneducated, lice infested, malnourished and undesirable man was one day walking on the streets of Kabale, his home town, when he looked in a mirror and was baffled at what he had become. For the first time in a long while, he got to see himself for who he really was. And it was at that moment that he heard the question, "Do you want to live or die?"

He considered his lot. He had nothing to his name. Yet he chose to live. He chose life. How I thank God that he chose life. Five years later just before he graduated from seminary, he committed his life to Jesus Christ and has walked in relationship with Him since then.

This same man would many years later turn out to be the biological father of Paulo Mugarura, one of my best friends, and a father to me in more ways than one. Uncle Ben has not only fathered me but a countless number of people in Uganda as well. I know you may think it an exaggeration when I say countless people but you need to come to Kampala and witness this for yourself.

Uncle Ben, as we fondly call him, is a retired Reverend Canon in the Anglican Church. He and his wife, Aunt Joy, have spent their lives fathering and mothering young people. They are the reason why numerous youth music groups like AYF, Heaven Bound, Destiny, Dove7, Voices of Victory, Come Alive Ministries (which later became Worship Harvest Ministries) and so many others existed. They are the reason why ministers like Ruth Nankabirwa and so many other dignitaries are in leadership. This couple is a legend. In their time as chaplain of St. Francis Chapel Makerere (1988-2007), they opened up their lives, their hearts, their home and their fridge to so many of us. I personally cannot count how much of their bread I ate as a young man.

Like it is in all families, every child has an 'oops' story that makes for good laughter when the family gathers and here is mine. I was seated at table with all the Mugaruras: Uncle Ben, Aunt Joy, Jackie, Gloria, Rachel, Paulo and Peter. Somehow they were always able to squeeze in an extra chair for me or anyone of the so many other young people that Uncle Ben and Aunt Joy called their own.

That day, they served some thick, flattened, dark brown things. Everyone picked one of the weird things except me. I was not going to get anything that ugly on my plate, let alone into my mouth. I was happy to eat my bun with a cup of tea. I was more comfortable dealing with what I knew well. The rest got this thing and added yellow and red stuff to it. I was unmoved and uninterested. They all tried to get me to try it but I was obstinate. After the meal, I asked what that stuff was.

Now in the Mugarura household, you had to quickly learn that no one escaped being teased. I think it was Rachel that figured it out first. I had failed to enjoy the full meal because I had never seen a beef burger! I remember them laughing so hard for quite a while. Then Jackie and Gloria somehow put an end to the laughter that had almost everyone in stitches. I laughed at myself too, yet still waiting to get an explanation. Aunt Joy explained what a beef burger was and from that day on, a beef burger is one of my favorite orders in any restaurant that I visit in the cities I have travelled to.

From Uncle Ben, I learnt how to lead a family, how to treat a wife with honor, how to make money and manage it with my wife and so much more. This previously undesirable man had many years later become a father to me because he embraced the love of God the Father.

Men can keep themselves immersed in an environment of fatherhood. We can keep ourselves learning from a God who is also a Father. It is always interesting to know that God is Love itself.

He who does not love does not know God, for God is love.

(1 John 4:8)

In the Bible, we see God being a doting parent who encourages, celebrates, strikes conversation, heals and protects His people. We also see Him challenge, chasten and rebuke while He forgives and envisions His people.

Here is an invaluable truth worth lots more than the price of this book:

You cannot be a great father without love.

You must be fully aware of the truth that God loves you in order for you to love your own children. If a car runs empty on fuel, it comes to a grinding halt. Fathering is based on love, fueled by love and sustained with love. If you can't love them, you can't father them.

This is how love is described;

Love suffers long and is kind; love does not envy; love does not parade itself, is not puffed up; does not behave rudely, does not seek its own, is not provoked, thinks no evil; does not rejoice in iniquity, but rejoices in the truth; bears all things, believes all things, hopes all things, endures all things. Love never fails. (1 Corinthians 13:4-8a)

If you are immersed in a love this great, it is easy to love like you are loved.

Men, fathers, gentlemen and fellow bearers of the mantle of fatherhood, I beseech you by the mercies of God, please consider embracing God's love for you today if you haven't yet. The hope of all nations is pegged on your being a great father and your only hope of being a great father is pegged on your being assured that you are loved by God.

Great fathers raise great families. Great families make great nations.

You are a critical piece in the transformation of our world. Your fathering role cannot be underestimated. Fathers are the reason we have Mandela, Obama or Hilter, the good, the bad or the ugly. Our role and our fathering responsibilities cannot be picked up by our wives, siblings, children or God, even when they badly want to.

You are the only father that your children will ever get to have. You are the only father that those who look up to you will ever have.

You must determine at this moment that you are going to be a really good father; a great father. You must decide to ignore all your messes and disdain the voices that condemn your past. You must decide to be shaped by a future you decide instead of a past you can't change. You must decide at this moment that you are going to be a real, present, life changing father.

You must decide today to always choose love.

Chapter Four: Fathering suffers long

29th November, 1985 is a day that went down in the annals of history. I guess the event did not make global news because the journalists of the day must have been napping or wasting time with little nothings, like the political bickering of the leaders of the day or government's peace talks with Museveni's guerrilla army.

I carried in my hands the most damning report.

I am an experiential learner. I like to explore things and experience them for myself. If there was a camp where I could experience all subjects in school by touch, taste, audio and visual stimuli, I would be the top of every class.

Unfortunately, my experiential self got into so much more trouble than I could handle.

I loved to play. While in Primary Four (Grade Three equivalent) at Buganda Road Primary School, I played so much in the dust that the dirt on me could have made a pig jealous. Buganda Road Primary School had white shirts and brown Khaki shorts for a school uniform. I always succeeded in making my uniform quite brown.

I used to get so dirty that later on when my mother was doing my shopping for secondary school, she got me a really brown towel and really brown bed sheets. There was little guessing what color a white towel would have had on my return after a term away in boarding school.

Back in Primary Four, I loved to eat fish.

In those days, road side vendors had started deep frying a type of fish called Nile Perch (Mpuuta). I guarantee that you too would have enjoyed this delicacy from Uganda, if you were a nine year old with my means.

My parents always gave me money to buy a break time snack at school. Sometimes I was also given money to take a taxi back home from school. That was a daily income.

I rarely bought snacks. Somehow, I made friends that always had more than enough to spare at break time. I was never a big eater anyway. So I almost routinely saved my snack money to buy fish.

One day on my way home, I bought a really hot piece of fish and could not eat it right away. I got a brilliant idea. I put the piece with its dripping oil in my shirt pocket and walked on, bent forward like an old man so it wouldn't burn me. Soon, it cooled off and I enjoyed it before I got home. The only problem was that my mother washed our school uniforms every evening upon our arrival. I clearly failed to explain away the fish oil in my shirt pocket.

It is for some of these events and more that both my parents kept admonishing me to be like my older brother, Ronnie. Ronnie is one of those very responsible, always-do-things-right, angelic type of brother. He never got as dirty as I did and was always doing his school work. He was even bigger and stronger than me such that when I got into a fist fight with him, it always led one way. I was always the vanquished and he the victor. In fact, many times he tried to avoid a fight because he felt sorry for me.

So I got despondent, being compared to Ronnie all the time. I am the second born of my mother and I am sure second born children relate with my plight. The people at school called me Ronnie's young brother. My parents at home kept admonishing me to be like Ronnie. I mostly dressed up in hand-downs from my brother. So at some point, I snapped.

I decided I was going to curve out a world for myself, different from the Ronnie world. I went about curving out the Chris world and boy, it was so much fun! I decided that since Ronnie is an ardent and keen student, I was going to do otherwise.

Whenever we were dropped at school with my cousins in their family Mazda, I would attend class only up to break time. I would thereafter find one of the many holes in the school wire-mesh fence and take off to enjoy my world. I kicked stones and watched all manner of movies free of charge. I would go to Norman Cinema (located at the current Watoto Church Downtown building), sneak in under the legs of adult men who had gone to watch and stayed hidden in the cinema as long as I wanted.

When I got tired of the movies, I went to City Nursery school, behind Kisozi house. Exactly where Kisozi house is, there was a huge plantation that had yellow flowers. To this day, I am not sure whether they were sunflowers or something else. What I am sure about is that this was my forest in my Chris world.

So I played a game (Cops and Robbers) with unwilling passers-by. It was akin to playing Robin Hood raiding royal estates and hiding in a forest. Only that this time, I threw stones at passersby. The infuriated strangers, totally miffed, would try to run and catch me. I would run into my turf, my forest, and disappear in there. I so mastered my craft that no single pursuant ever caught up with me. That was my world and I enjoyed it for a whole year.

Fred Sebidde Kiryowa (Now an editor with the New Vision newspaper in Uganda) was one of my good friends. For a reason I can't recall, we had an early release from school one day. Fred lived in the neighborhood and decided to return a visit in exchange for the numerous visits I had paid him before then. Unknown to me, I was like a frog swimming in steadily warming water. Fred had carried his school bag!

My mother greeted him and quickly struck a school conversation. He had always been a good natured lad so he got into it pretty quickly. Unfortunately, Fred did not know that the more he spoke of his exploits and how much work he had to carry home, the more trouble I sank into.

My mother asked to have a look at his books and she was in shock. She compared them to mine and the truth was there for all to see.

I had one 48-page book for each subject. Fred had three to four books folded and bound together using newspaper covers.

I was embarrassed and cross with Fred all at the same time. By just being him, he had landed me into quite some serious trouble.

I definitely told a lie about losing my books and reasoned that additionally, Fred's handwriting had larger letters than mine; thus more pages were used for notes.

For some reason, my mother did not press me hard for answers and I got off the hook. However, I was not two times lucky.

The year-end promotion examinations were scheduled and I had to sit for them. There was no way I could miss those ones. That moment is as fresh now as it was then. As I filed past the teacher, into the examination room for my Math paper, I heard my classmates speak about Roman numerals.

I wondered what on earth they were talking about. They said the Student teacher, Mr. Lubega, had said the examination would be worked out in Arabic numerals but all answers were to be given in Roman numerals.

I calmly asked, "What are Roman Numerals?"

My shocked classmates swung into action. I believe some were trying to help but the others were taking advantage of my misery for their final practice. "Number one is i, Two is ii, Three is iii, Four is iv and five v," gleefully yelled one of my classmates. I asked what ten was and the answer X only riveted me with fear and increased my panic and trembling. I was already in the examination room. I could not redeem this one.

A few weeks later, when the end of year report was handed to me, I was sure that I had done badly but not to the same estimation of my teachers. I read the class teacher's verdict and at once knew how terrible a lashing I was going to receive.

My classmates had been promoted to P.5.

I had been demoted to P.3.

That was the report I carried back home on 29th November, 1985. Everyone in my class knew how badly I had performed. In Buganda Road Primary School, all the names and all the results were clearly shown on everyone's report. There was no hiding. I had to deliver a report where a girl called Peace Kabagambe had topped the class with stellar marks and I was at the rock bottom, even performing worse than some students who had missed some examinations.

That day, my walk back home seemed to take eons. I devised a plan to deliver the report but play hide and seek with my father that whole evening. He played along. I actually believed that I had escaped his wrath. I finally got into bed and woke up to the tap of my father's hand on my shoulder at 6:30am the next morning. He asked me to dress up and meet him in the backyard. I obliged, somehow convinced that he had forgotten about my report.

My father had spent the previous evening slow-roasting two debarked canes, freshly cut off a pine tree. He got me to calculate how much money of his that I had squandered that year. I told you my father is good at accounts. This is partly how I know. We did the annual calculation and then multiplied it by two considering I had just lost two years. It was an enormous figure so we agreed to remove the zeros and use the first two digits. There it was: 15 cuts of the cane.

The style he used to administer them was one where you received a lecture, a cut of the cane, then you ran around the compound to cool off. Shortly after, another lecture started yet another cycle.

My father was furious.

When he gave me the last five cuts of the cane like rapid machine gun-fire, I was yelling but not really crying. Much as they felt painful, they were well within my threshold of pain tolerance.

Angered by my unexpected response, he tagged at my shirt to kick my backside for good measure. I dodged the kick. As I made an attempt to get away, my shirt got torn. He then said in our mother tongue that I was stupid, considering I had not even cried after such a lashing.

It's at that point that I cried like a baby.

I cried because the shirt was new, a gift from my Aunt Edith (my mum's younger sister, whom I loved). I also cried because he called me stupid. That hurt a lot.

Knowing what my father had put up with, he really had suffered long with me. I too would probably be at my wit's end.

I painted for you the picture of what type of child I was. I bet you would not want to deal with a child like I was. Yet even after this incident, my father still continued to pay my school fees and give me money for the break time snack. He painfully saw me go through P.3 and P.4 all over again.

Do you have a problem child? It might be that this child has been a thorn in your flesh since they learnt how to walk. They could have sliced and diced all six of your leather dining chairs like I did. They could be living a promiscuous life, chosen a sexual orientation you distaste, dragged your name in the mud, robbed the bank fifty times over, been in and out of jail and made you sick with high blood pressure or something worse in the process.

Do not give up on your child. It is only your goodness toward them that will lead them back on the right path. Your love for them is the only language that will pierce through their hardened hearts.

My father put up a lot with me. I was so playful that I had somehow managed to blow up a two years' education investment. I have heard of men who disown their children on such accounts. I recently realized how my father's not disowning me was part of his suffering long with me. He could have. Instead, he continued to pay my school fees and making sure I had food on my plate and a roof over my head.

Suffering long has those two words for a reason. Yes we know you are suffering. Yes, we agree it has been long. But please don't give up on your own. Love them out of their wrong. It is exactly what Father God does for us.

Or do you despise the riches of His goodness, forbearance, and longsuffering, not knowing that the goodness of God leads you to repentance? (Romans 2:4)

That same goodness of God is in you as a father. Use it generously on your wayward child.

Chapter Five: Fathering is kind

One of my earliest recollections of a mosquito net was when my father was putting me under one. I must have been four years old. I almost remember every kind thing my father has done for me.

When I was six years old, I had a fever and ran a very high temperature. I felt so bad and passed out for a moment. My father must have been in the shower when my mother called for his help. I temporarily gained consciousness and saw him carry me in his arms.

I passed out again.

After I gained consciousness, my mother told me that my father had rushed me to the garage and drove me to Mengo Hospital while wrapped in a towel. He actually hit his face hard against a sharp end of an open window, got a wound, bled, but ignored his pain to save my life. He still bears that scar of love for me. Fathers are kind, caring and sympathetic.

My daughter Sinza seems to always get this side of a father out of me. She is so sensitive to there being perfect harmony between us that when she doubts it, I have to gently hug her and reassure her. I do not think it petty and soft because I am a man.

Society has conditioned men to be macho. We have taken on this conditioning and believed this stereotype in many cases much to our detriment.

Some of the toughest, meanest men ever have also been known to be caring, gentle and protective of their children. Stories are told about how Field Marshal Idi Amin Dada, sometimes called the butcher of Africa, was a doting father.

The ruthlessness and care all wrapped up in one package of a man is perplexing and a paradox that we struggle to comprehend. If a man like Idi Amin could somehow afford to care for his children so can you.

There is no point in acting macho to win the praise of men and lose a vital relationship with your child.

You will actually be shocked at how gentle and caring God the Father can be. He uses motherly language like brooding over his people like a hen. He says we are the apple of His eye. He uses a picture of carrying His people on eagles' wings. That is a female eagle's job. She is the one who raises them up and teaches them how to fly.

'You have seen what I did to the Egyptians, and how I bore you on eagles' wings and brought you to Myself'. (Exodus 19:4)

My wife, Lynnet, tells stories about how tough her father was. She and her siblings made sure all his meals were ready on time. They tiptoed into his presence and dashed out at the earliest opportunity.

He was an astute man and a keen time keeper. When he was the manager at Uganda Electricity Board (UEB) in Kampala, he had the keys to both the Kampala office and the Lugogo power station. He somehow managed to open both offices and still be the first man at either place. In the chaotic seventies and eighties in Uganda, we needed some consistent and reliable men like him in order to have electricity.

He was so thorough that when you watched him do his shoe laces, it looked like a whole engineering operation. It was precision engineering at its best. The bows he tied were neat and always equivalent.

When she was a little older, Lynnet had to deal with her dad more, especially after her mum travelled to work in Canada. She realized that they had grown up believing a lie. Her father was gentle, caring, warm and funny. He had actually been one of the funny men on Radio Uganda in his hay days. He played immaculate classical music on the guitar.

I experienced him first hand for 10 years before he passed away on 27th December, 2010. If Engineer Steven Karebi was anything, he was a caring man.

Once when one of his sons was expelled from school, he did not condemn him and speak down at him. He looked for a way to plug him back into another good school and give him a chance at life. That's who he was; a very caring and non judgmental man.

It was later discovered after his passing that he was the one who always looked out for people in his extended family. He fathered children that were beyond his biological children. He took care of people.

I remember the day I first met him. I had escorted my girlfriend to visit her siblings in King's College Budo and found her dad there. I greeted him and we got chatting. There was always a feeling of safety around him. It did not matter who you were. When he accepted you as a child, he cared for you.

He let me stay overnight three times in his house before I had even married his daughter. In Africa, that is rare. At the introduction ceremony, before our wedding, he refused to cave in to his relatives' pressure to charge me bride price. I married from Ankole in Western Uganda. That meant that I had to come up with very many cows in order to marry the girl I loved. He said to me in private that I did not need to worry about bride price. All he wanted was for me to love his daughter.

This man really cared for me. He knew that I was of very simple means. He accepted me just as I was. He was gentle with me. He drew me out and allowed me to offload the pain on my heart. He helped me work through the deep pains and agonies in my heart. He had a big heart that could carry the burden of others.

I spent every Christmas with him after our wedding in July 2004. He was my father and my friend. Many times, he would call me to just chat with me. My wife would wonder at the fact that he had not asked after her. He just wanted to speak to me. His home in Mbarara was my stop for deep wisdom.

So when he was ill, I was one of the people at the forefront of fighting to save his life. He loved me and cared for me deeply. How else was I to respond when my father was ill?

Chapter Six: Fathering does not rejoice in iniquity

One of the men I have had the honor of being fathered by is Apostle John Bunjo.

The first time I met him, he was a young man, probably only ten years my senior. He was a different type of young man.

He always carried about him the sense of someone who was going to become something big in life.

He had a sense of urgency about him. He was a hilarious and incisive preacher.

I remember how he introduced himself in one of the very early sermons he preached at Church of the Redeemed Apostles (CORA). He spoke in Luganda and said, "My name is Siraje Bunjo the son of Hajji Abdu Kyekulidde."

He had come to faith in Jesus Christ and his father, a Muslim, had thrown him out of home because of his newfound faith.

At the point I met him, he was staying in the servant quarters of the house that also doubled as the church.

David and Jessica Sekyeru had started this church in the compound of their home. They were, and still are, business people that wanted to make a difference in the lives of their community through the gospel. They were not really the teaching pastors of the church. They opened up the space for people like Paul Musuula, James Mwesigwa, James Katumba and John Bunjo.

Even as he was cutting his teeth in preaching at crusades and quickly becoming a much sought-after preacher, John Bunjo was a father at heart. It was in this time that he changed his name from Siraje to John. Being rejected by his father must have dug a deep well of fathering in him.

He often visited to check on us in a little two bed roomed house in Najjanankumbi that my brother and I called the White House.

In a season when my father was not available, John Bunjo fathered me. He asked after me, checked on me in Sunday school and celebrated my achievements. There is a time when my mother, my brother and I acted in a church drama and he was so impressed with my performance. He was generous with his compliments.

What stood out about John Bunjo is that he had no kind words for sin or iniquity. Chief among the iniquities he despised was sex out of marriage. It was not uncommon for him to find you on the village path, greet you and ask, *"Zippu okyagisibye?"* meaning, "Is your zip still up?"

This man had suffered a lot for believing in Jesus. He did not see why anyone should pay such a high price then mess with the treasure of salvation.

He too was a hot blooded young man but I guess he did not understand how people can be given to sin galore.

One of his famous statements was, *"Nze nkyawa ekibi,"* meaning, "I hate sin."

This is also the testimony about Jesus.

But to the Son He says:

"Your throne, O God, is forever and ever; A scepter of righteousness is the scepter of Your kingdom.

You have loved righteousness and hated lawlessness; Therefore God, Your God, has anointed You With the oil of gladness more than Your companions."

(Hebrews 1:8-9)

Jesus loved righteousness and hated lawlessness. One could mistakenly imagine that He walked around like a religious bigot with pomp and splendor with His nose pointing to the sky, looking down upon the sinners around him. But He was not like that. He spent so much time with sinners that the religious class of His day disdainfully labeled Him a friend of sinners.

One of Jesus' most fatherly acts was when a young woman who had thoroughly messed up was brought to Him. He did not judge her and neither did he celebrate her sin. He got rid of those who condemned her and admonished her to go and sin no more.

But Jesus went to the Mount of Olives. Now early in the morning He came again into the temple, and all the people came to Him; and He sat down and taught them. Then the scribes and Pharisees brought to Him a woman caught in adultery. And when they had set her in the midst, they said to Him, "Teacher, this woman was caught in adultery, in the very act. Now Moses, in the law, commanded us that such should be stoned. But what do You say?" This they said, testing Him, that they might have something of which to accuse Him. But Jesus stooped down and wrote on the ground with His finger, as though He did not hear.

So when they continued asking Him, He raised Himself up and said to them, "He who is without sin among you, let him throw a stone at her first." And again He stooped down and wrote on the ground. Then those who heard it, being convicted by their conscience, went out one by one, beginning with the oldest even to the last. And Jesus was left alone, and the woman standing in the midst. When Jesus had raised Himself up and saw no one but the woman, He said to her, "Woman, where are those accusers of yours? Has no one condemned you?"

She said, "No one, Lord."

And Jesus said to her, "Neither do I condemn you; go and sin no more." (John 8:1-11)

It is possible to love in such a way as to encourage right and discourage wrong.

It is possible to father in such a way as to drive away sin and have an abundance of righteous living.

John Bunjo did that. He encouraged all the right around me and discouraged the things that could have totally changed the script of my life.

I graduated from Sunday school under this man's watchful eye. He must have noticed that some girls that we graduated with into the adult church were already sexually active. That is something one can't hide.

We knew it and hoped the leaders did not because we thought these girls would get into lots of trouble. We were all classmates but they lived different lives.

One time, one of the older church girls was quite overt with her pursuit. First she tried my brother and he ran for dear life. I was next in line and this time I copied my brother and fled.

Sam Ewau, a famous preacher in the Scripture Union fellowship circles of our days, describes fleeing as something between flying and running.

The leaders must have been so concerned about what was going on that one day, one of the leaders, a father to a girl in Sunday school, sat me through a long lecture that was insulating his daughter from any advances from me. I honestly never had such designs and I remember really being offended by his assertions and suspicions. We were just friends.

Such was the treachery of our youthful days.

John Bunjo took on a different approach. He did not judge and neither did he rejoice in iniquity. He called it what it was: sin. Just like Jesus did. Most importantly however, John Bunjo called out the righteousness in me. He always lovingly called me his son and whenever he introduced me, he spoke about me as his son who was still a virgin.

Those were the early nineties. Fourteen years later on 24th July, 2004, I married Lynnet and had white socks on. I had promised myself that if I made it to my wedding as a virgin; I would put on white socks.

I remember my dad being absolutely stunned at my putting on white socks on a black suit. My dad is British-trained and a sharp dresser. I never got a chance to apologize for my wardrobe malfunction. I will take this chance to say, Sorry Dad.

I did not have the proper dress etiquette on my wedding day but John Bunjo had successfully fathered me by celebrating righteousness in me and teaching me to hate iniquity. I can say that he succeeded in teaching me that fornication was sin.

I have met him a couple of times over the years and I remember meeting him when he was still associate pastor at Victory Christian Centre Ndeeba. I walked into his office and before all the pleasantries he asked me, "Is your zip still up?"

Chapter Seven: Fathering rejoices in truth

In a very tense moment when the court was silent and the accused had fired back three shots in response to questions that were potent enough to incriminate Him, the judge asked a heavy question.

"What is truth?"

Moments later the crowd went wild and bayed for His blood. He was handed to the executioners and the rest is the famous story of the crucifixion of Jesus.

It is Pontius Pilate's question that still begs for an answer.

"What is truth?"

While praying for His disciples, Jesus asked this

of the Father.

Sanctify them by Your truth. Your word is truth. (John 17:17)

God's word is truth. That is the strict definition of truth. God puts so much weight on His word that He has placed His word above His fame, above His reputation and above the power that His name carries.

I will worship toward Your holy temple, and praise Your name for Your loving kindness and Your truth; for You have magnified Your word above all Your name. (Psalm 138:2)

It is said that a man's word is his gold. Fathers essentially create worlds by their words.

Have you ever stopped to think that your children are actually a product of your words, not just your sperm?

You spoke words of endearment to your wife. She fell in love with you. You hopefully married her. You consummated your love. And lo and behold: children!

Sperm with no love usually takes the form of rape and many unseemly scenarios we would rather not paint.

It starts with words. It always starts with words.

She believes you because when she checks them out, there is truth in them. We can never underestimate truth and words.

A man who is a serial borrower and never pays back soon runs out of options to borrow.

I once had someone ask me to lend him some money. I didn't have the kind of cash that he wanted but I thought I could recommend him to a friend in the money lending business with whom, I had a very good reputation. When I mentioned this fellow's name, my friend let out the chuckle of a hard hearted skeptic on the other end of the phone. He told me in no uncertain terms that there is no way he could lend the fellow any money. This fellow had borrowed from the whole network of money lenders in the city and failed to keep his word to pay his loans. They had talked to each other and blacklisted him. It is only the powerful office he held in government that kept him from going to jail.

When God says something, it will happen. His word is gold. You can bank on God's word

"For as the rain comes down, and the snow from heaven, And do not return there, But water the earth, And make it bring forth and bud, That it may give seed to the sower And bread to the eater, So shall My word be that goes forth from My mouth; It shall not return to Me void, But it shall accomplish what I please, And it shall prosper in the thing for which I sent it. (Isaiah 55:10-11)

I believe that this is the same standard to which our word ought to be as fathers. We need to weigh carefully through what we say, how we say it and who we say it to.

The words of a father are truth to his children.

This is part of what makes fatherhood a really heavy responsibility.

Your children tend to believe everything you say; it is only when they find your words inconsistent and dishonest that they stop believing. Sadly at this stage, they throw out everything you have to say. You are not taken seriously from that point on, no matter what. It takes only God's redemptive work to repair such a scenario.

When I was 10 years old, my father took me out for lunch in town to a little restaurant on William Street in Kampala.

At the beginning of the meal, I noticed that the beef did not have enough salt seasoning. I picked up the salt shaker and applied its contents generously. My father let me go on. When I was satisfied that the taste was to my liking, I went about the business of devouring my meal.

Then he said, "It is not good to add uncooked salt to your food. It is not healthy."

To this day, I do not know the scientific facts that back up his words but I struggle to add uncooked salt to my food. This is true even when I am sprinkling salt on the obvious, like a boiled egg. I still hear my father's words.

At the end of the meal, I used a tooth pick and got up from the table with it in my mouth. My father said, "It is not good to walk around with a tooth pick in your mouth. It does not look proper."

Since then, I have not managed to successfully walk away from a table with a tooth pick in my mouth. Even when I do, I immediately break it and throw it away when I remember my father's words.

As fathers, our words shape the world of our children.

It is not uncommon to hear people say "My father said..." Fathers are unpublished authorities. A father does not have to be a college professor to be quoted by his children. It is his love for them that makes him an authority as far as they are concerned.

God must have wired things this way so that fathers are able to teach and discipline their children. I know that for many African men the word discipline paints the picture of spanking a child. I hope that from the little story of the meal I had with my father, you can see discipline without the cane.

When I was eight years old, my father promised to buy me a brand new bicycle if I performed well in school. We agreed on a target and I hit it. My father never bought me that bicycle.

It was the most painful of experiences. I reminded him but for some reason it never materialized.

I have since tried to reason with myself saying, "Maybe he had no money, but he really did not mean to break his promise."

I am a grown man. I have two kids. I have bought them bicycles. Yet the little boy in me still longs for a bicycle from my father.

I know that sounds outrageous. But before you write me off as a psychiatric case, I want you to know that I let go of that promise. If my dad bought me a bicycle now, it would not be the same thing. I just wish, within me, that he had bought that bicycle. It would have helped me hold up his word more than I did after that incident.

Life did not help matters later on, when I went to talk to my father about paying my school fees. He would promise to do so, genuinely believing that a deal would come through. When it didn't, I was crushed and kept building a case of the unreliability of his word, which started from the bicycle incident.

That one area was a source of bitterness toward my father for many years. I eventually got over it but it hurt while it lasted.

Many years later, as a father, I too make promises to our children. Because of the pain I experienced, I try to keep the promises the best I can. Some promises, however, are tough to keep.

In 2011, I was due for my Masters' graduation from the East and Southern Africa Management Institute (ESAMI) in Arusha, Tanzania.

In my excitement, as my family and I spoke about what we hoped for at the beginning of the year, I mentioned a desire to travel with them for the graduation in late November that year. We would stay there for Lemuel's sixth birthday.

The way the year turned out financially was totally unexpected and what happened was unprecedented. Uganda, for the first time since the mid 1980's, experienced double-digit inflation.

In a bid to curb this phenomenon, the Governor of Bank of Uganda, Emmanuel Tumusiime Mutebile, raised the interbank lending rate to reduce how much money was in circulation in the economy. That one move also increased the commercial bank lending rates.

My wife and I had taken out a mortgage from Stanbic Bank to complete our first house. That house had lots of sentimental attachments and we spared nothing good, including a sizeable mortgage, on it.

At that time, I had a steady long-term consultancy job with the World Bank and we hoped to pay the loan off quickly. But we did not know the difference between fixed lending rates and flexible lending rates.

We had a flexible rate loan. Never negotiate for this type
of loan.

The terms and conditions in the fine print meant that the bank could raise its lending rate without consulting its clients. At some point the lending rate rose from 15% to 29% in a few weeks!

That is even higher than the profit margin of many credible businesses!

So we found ourselves paying through the nose to pull off the monthly bank payments.

Around August that year, our children's excitement about going to Arusha reached fever pitch. It was all they spoke about.

I had also made a promise to another man I honor, Dr. Moses Isooba, that we would be visiting with his family while in Arusha. Our relationship was young and budding. It was important that I did not flip-flop. Once again, I had given my word.

In the meantime, at the end of August, I found out I was not going to graduate that year. We had travelled with my wife to London for Marriage Course training in June that same year and I had missed more than three days of my law lectures. ESAMI does not allow you to seat for any examinations in such a scenario. I had to find a law class for that paper and the next was being offered by ESAMI in Lusaka, Zambia the next year.

The critical question was to go or not to go to Arusha in 2011.

This became part of my late night discussions with my wife and my day time consultations with many of my friends. There was a lot of back and forth yet in my heart of hearts my mind had already been made up. I was going to be a father who honored my word and kept my promise to my children.

We found a way of flying to Arusha with the kids. This too was their very first time to fly.

I remember visiting some of my classmates in Arusha and they were all shocked that I flew to Arusha even when I had not made it to the graduation list. It was the most confusing of happenings for them. I admit it was for me too, yet I was glad I did not break my promise. I kept my word.

We eventually sold our house in 2013, got out of that terrible debt scenario and started rebuilding our net worth.

I am really glad that my trust net worth with my son and daughter are still intact. A father's word is his gold. It is true for God; it is true for you.

Your words create. Words sanctify. God's words sanctify and so do yours.

Sanctify them by Your truth. Your word is truth. (John 17:17)

There are so many men that I have met, who soar upon the words of their father, or are crushed and kept prisoners of life because of their father's words.

I struggled under the weight of my father's words when he, in anger, said, "You are stupid!"

From that day, it became my single-minded objective to prove him wrong. I studied hard, topped my class and, when I did badly, I was never out of the top ten.

I was fighting words that had been spoken and long forgotten.

I know my dad loves me and I love him very much, but I am truthfully narrating these experiences with a hope that this will give your children a chance to be fathered better than most of the experiences our generation has had.

I got four distinctions in my Primary Leaving Examinations and joined Kings College Budo. I did quite well through my years there although I had a poor finish in my senior four. I got 16 points in 6 subjects and 22 points in 8 subjects. I was exported to Mwiri where I did not perform well. I got only one principle pass in my advanced level certificate examinations.

With the help of my father, I was enrolled for a certificate in banking at the Institute of Banking and was one of the best. I later sat for mature age entry exams in 2003 and was the best in my category. I joined Makerere University on government sponsorship. I did well and got a cumulative grade point average of 4.4. I had an upper second honors degree.

All this while, through the highs and the lows, I wanted to prove to my father that I was not stupid.

These were wasted years, wasted efforts. I know he knows that I am not stupid. I know he knows that I am one of his brightest children. I know he knows it.

So what was the fuss all about?

Words! His words!

How different it would have been if he had said, "I am disappointed by the results you have brought home but I know you can do better."

There is no knowing. Only God knows. All I know is that I can do better with my words over my children and so can you. We can create an excellent, victorious, loving, confident and reassured future for them with our words.

It takes a few seconds to tell a child, 'I love you', 'I believe in you', 'You are the best!'

It takes a few seconds, yet it changes the very course of their future and history.

Fathers, please be generous with your positive words over your children. What you speak is truth. If you tell your child that he will build the first hospital on the moon, it costs you nothing. There is no knowing what the fire you have started in their belly can achieve.

I pray that you will speak words that build. I pray that you will live by the words you speak. I pray that you will keep the promises you make so that you can teach your children to be like you. It is only then that you will have the moral authority to teach truth.

A few weeks ago, I promised some first time guests at Worship Harvest Church, Gayaza, that I would visit them during the week.

My wife and I pastor that congregation.

So during the next week I had to keep my word. I am not yet forty years old yet this couple is approaching their late seventies. The wonder of fathering is that in this case, as the pastor of the congregation, I am a father even to them.

So I picked a day and set out to look for them. Incidentally, it was also my day to spend time with Lemuel, so off we went.

We looked for this couple's home using the directions they gave us and found it but they were not there.

The guards at the gate kept pointing us to different locations where this couple could be. We made three attempts and as we drove on to make the fourth attempt, my son asked, "Daddy, must we see these people?"

I grabbed the teaching opportunity. I explained to him that I had given my word and had to keep it.

If I were a regular at not keeping my word, there is no way I would have had an opportunity to teach it to my son.

Concerning the truth and concerning your word: Speak it, keep it, live it and teach it.

Chapter Eight: Fathering in Silence and Prayer

My maternal Grandfather, Ernest Ssentongo Kibalama, had a loud voice. Though he shared a bedroom with his wife, they slept on different beds. This bedroom was like a World War II command post. It was the only way to cope and manage their full house. They had twelve children and the house was full of hustle and bustle. Their beds were the launch pads of so many instructions, which their large brood had to adhere to.

Both my maternal Grandfather and Grandmother were not much educated but I must applaud them for keeping tabs on my mother and her siblings. They were so good at this role that their children to this day call them Commander and Commandess.

My Grandfather was eight years old when he was rushed from school to go see his father. His father was a mechanic and a thoroughbred drunkard. He arrived to find his father in a critical condition, frothing around his mouth. The locals applied the only treatment they knew for an alcoholic man in that state. My grandfather found men and women peeing in his father's mouth. That was the last day he saw his father alive.

He and his brother were looked after by relatives but never really got a chance to go back to school.

My grandfather loved education and hated alcohol.

He did all in his power to educate his children and he succeeded. If they needed anything from him, the way to pitch the sale was to give it an educational angle. He always said yes to education.

He never touched alcohol all his life and he admonished his children not to do so. None of his children that were given to alcohol have had an admirable life.

His commanding exploits notwithstanding, my grandfather lived a life that speaks volumes like a billboard. His way of life and achievements were there for all to see yet he never once bragged about them.

He fathered me in silence and prayer.

My earliest recollection of being outside my grandfather's home was in 1979 when I was barely three years old.

The Tanzanian soldiers and Ugandan rebels were marching into Kampala along the dusty road in front of his home in two files. Some had one gun and others had two. Idi Amin Dada, the self-proclaimed life president of Uganda, had been deposed.

We had left the house and were hiding in a potato garden. Those days were uncertain. There was no knowing who the good or bad guys were. A few days earlier I had banged my mouth on the dining table. I later found out that that was the effect of the Saba Saba, a heavy artillery gun that dropped bombshells which shook the ground. My grandfather's house got a crack in the kitchen wall which has somehow kept its place to this day.

I am not sure where my father was at the time of this war. All I know is that it was at my grandfather's that we took refuge.

My earliest recollection of my grandfather seems to be the thread of what he meant to me in both his life and his death. His home was a place of refuge.

Whenever there was tension at home, he came and took us away. I have a feeling that I could have been exposed to much more back at home had it not been for the refuge that my grandfather was to us.

I remember coming by taxi with him from town and alighting in Katwe. He always walked from Katwe to Lukuli, Nanganda, where his home was. Those five kilo metres were precious. As we walked, I could sometimes feel like I connected to his heart and his thoughts. He was quite meditative in those days.

He was both my grandfather and my father too. His silence usually calmed my nerves. His presence always said to me, "Things will be okay."

There are men who are not loud, who do not have charm or lots of stories to tell. It is important that they too know that they can be great fathers.

Sometimes silence is golden. Sometimes a child does not need anyone to be talking or explaining away the challenges of life. Sometimes all they need is your presence, a firm, assuring hold, a smile and eyes that hear what is going on in their heart. Being with my grandfather made me feel like his eyes could hear what was going on in my heart.

I would have that kind of day with him then he would call me to his room in the evening to pray. He always sang the Luganda version of the hymn, "Abide with me." The other hymn was "Jjo ne leero." I do not know its English version.

I have two pictures of my grandfather: him walking with me and on his knees praying for me and others.

He seemed to always be doing that. In the last seven years of his life, he was mostly bedridden. But whenever he could afford it, he knelt down to pray.

I cannot explain why I loved my grandfather so dearly. I cannot quote him. I cannot point to things that interest children like circuses that he took me to. What I remember are the walks, his firm, assuring hand holding mine, the understanding look and the prayers.

He lost the battle to multiple ailments in August 1994. I was eighteen years old when he died. I hoped it was a bad joke. I hoped for one more walk, one more prayer and one more hold by him. The curtain had closed on his life but not on his fathering over me.

This way of fathering, though lacking in charisma, might be one of the best ways to father.

Uncle Ben Mugarura is another of the fathers who does this so well. Any of his children is assured of a bear hug, a listening ear and an understanding look. When he speaks, every word weighs heavy because his words aren't too many. I also know him to be a prayerful man. There is no gift like the gift of being covered in prayer by your father.

Most of the other aspects on fathering that I learnt from my grandfather were passed on through stories I heard from my mother and others.

Because he loved to read, my grandfather, who was a janitor at Uganda bookshop, would quickly finish mopping the floor and cleaning the toilets and head to the bookshelves. If anyone was looking for him, they knew where to find him. He was always sandwiched by the bookshelves, reading a book.

One day, the accounts clerk decided not to come back to work. My grandfather, whose favorite section was accounts, asked to be given a chance to keep the books. He excelled so much at it that he did that same job for over thirty years.

I have had a very tumultuous time getting through my education. It was never because I was a poor student. It was my very adventurous spirit, the lack of stability at home and my passions that are to blame. I know, for example, that my abysmal academic performance in my Senior Four can be traced back to the 1994 FIFA World cup in Atlanta USA. The soccer matches were screened so late in the night that we had to keep awake to watch them. As late as 4am, I was up watching a match even when I had a mock examination at 9am that morning. That was ungoverned passion.

Everyone has a nemesis in class and mine was a tall guy called Ogenga. I had to beat Ogenga in class or I would die. In the mocks, Ogenga beat me and I gave up fighting. I gave up in the final Senior Four term.

In A level, I wanted to study Mathematics Economics and Geography. I loved commerce and accounts. I knew I'd love economics. I also did geography in my sleep. To this day, I have a natural compass and never lose my way. The school said they did not have any way for me to do such a course combination, so I was offered Physics Economics and Mathematics. I was dejected but did it anyway.

Then in my first term of Senior Five, our class teacher, who was also my mathematics teacher, threw me a punch that was below the belt. I asked a question and he quipped, "Do boys from Budo also ask such questions?"

That was it for me. I know it was stupid of me but I decided never to step into his class. I took offense and it cost me.

For the next 5 terms I never sat in a mathematics class and, obviously, my physics also suffered because mechanics is done in both mathematics and physics. I only attended the economics class which was taught by Mr. Murana, one of the best economics teachers in the world.

When my Uganda Advanced Certificate of Education results came out, I did not argue with them. I had BOO (B in economics, O in maths and O in physics). I keep joking that I was booed.

So went my academic life.

I estimate that by the time I started my University education, my friend, Fred Sebidde Kiryowa, with whom I had been in P.4 the first time must have been in gainful employment for five years.

Being eight years behind my peers academically did not
faze me.

I had a grandfather who had taught himself into a good job beyond what anyone would have thought.

I have actually done most of my studying as a 'Mature student' (too old for one's class) by self learning.

I read by myself and discuss the subject with a few people until I get it. That resilience came from my grandfather. I now have an MBA and would like to keep learning. I want to be a student for life.

My grandfather was also an astute business man. Somehow between his job and getting home, he exported African drums to Europe and made a killing while at it.

He was quite wealthy by the time he died. At some point in his last seven years, money from his property investments paid three full-time nurses who worked in 8-hour shifts every day in order to keep him alive.

My grandfather's business acumen started a fire in me. I am not where I want to be but I am on my way. Business and I are going to dance for a long time before my grave.

What amazes me the most is my grandfather fathered me in silence both in his life and in his death. It's the things he did that left an indelible mark on me. It's his prayer for me and the sound of my name that are the only audible parts of him that I have in my memory chest.

With silence and prayer he fathered me, leaving a huge impact on me.

In silence and prayer you can father your own children.

Chapter Nine: Fathering with Invitation and Challenge

I recently took a cursory look at eight generations of Americans born between 1912 and 2012. It made for an interesting read. Each generation over these one hundred years seemed to go to unhealthy extremes in a bid to correct the errors of their fathers. Additionally, each generation that came after seemed to lose the solid values that hold society together and build true wealth and prosperity.

The Depression Era generation (born: 1912-1921) were out to correct financial wrongs that they suffered. According to William J. Schroer12, these individuals tended to be conservative, compulsive savers. They maintained low debt and used more secure financial products like Certificates of Deposit versus stocks. They tended to feel a responsibility to leave a legacy to their children. They were patriotic, oriented toward work before pleasure, had respect for authority and a sense of moral obligation. This is the generation that had the values necessary to build true wealth. They saved, borrowed less, invested wisely, had a good work ethic and thought about legacy. They valued family, avoided self aggrandizement.

The World War II generation (born: 1922-1927) has people who shared a common goal of defeating the Axis of powers. The Axis of Powers was a group of countries that opposed the Allied powers in World War II, including Germany, Italy, and Japan as well as Bulgaria, Hungary, Romania, and Yugoslavia. This generation had an accepted sense of "deferment" postponement of pleasure in contrast with the emphasis on "me" in more recent generations. Their thrust seemed to be getting rid of bullies. Most of the positive values of the earlier generation were beginning to give way apart from postponing pleasure.

The Post-War generation (born: 1928-1945) had a value for security, comfort, and familiar, known activities and environments. You would imagine this possible especially after a war because everything is thrown into upheaval. Listening to T. Harv Ekker's audio (Secrets of a millionaire mind) quickly reveals to you that the middle class thinks about comfort not wealth. The American public at this time settled for the middle class life in contrast to having a wealthy mindset. I do not know about you but that looks like a down grade to me.

Boomers I or The Baby Boomers (born: 1946-1954) had good economic opportunities and were largely optimistic about the potential for America and their own lives, the Vietnam War notwithstanding.

This generation is unrecognizable to the depression era generation. They were focused on just making the money. This is the generation that began being 'me' focused. It only got worse in the generations that followed. It is no wonder that their fathering of generation X was terrible and miserable. You just need to see it to believe it. I find it interesting that the indicators of America's generations are very close to what happened elsewhere in the world. Thousands of miles away in Africa, in Uganda, this generation acted quite the same from what I can tell. Boomers II or Generation Jones (born: 1955-1965) faced economic struggles including the oil embargo of 1979 which reinforced a sense of "I'm out for me" and narcissism and a focus on self-help and skepticism over media and institutions. While Boomers I had the Vietnam war, Boomers II had AIDS as part of their rites of passage. The focus on me, myself and I only got worse with this generation.

Generation X (born: 1966-1976) is sometimes referred to as the "lost" generation, this was the first generation of "latchkey" kids, exposed to lots of daycare and divorce. According to Wikipedia, a latchkey child is a child who returns from school to an empty home because their parent or parents are away at work, or a child who is often left at home with little parental supervision.

Gen X is often characterized by high levels of skepticism, "what's in it for me" attitudes and a reputation for some of the worst music to ever gain popularity. William Morrow cited the childhood divorce of many Gen Xers as "one of the most decisive experiences influencing how Gen Xers shape their own families".

With an education higher than other generations and a growing maturity, they formed families with a higher level of caution and pragmatism than their parents demonstrated. Concerns run high over avoiding broken homes, kids growing up without a parent around and financial planning. This generation is seeking to correct the upheaval left by the Baby Boomers.

Generation Y, Echo Boomers or Millennials (born: 1977- 1994) are known as incredibly sophisticated technology-wise, immune to most traditional marketing and sales pitches as they not only grew up with it all, they've seen it all and been exposed to it all since early childhood. Gen Y kids often raised in dual income or single parent families have been more involved in family purchases, everything from groceries to new cars. One in nine Gen Y'ers has a credit card co-signed by a parent.

The boomers II fathered generation Y. Their egotistic outlook and self focus produced a generation that not only experienced divorce but also started the phenomenon of single parenting; children growing up with a single mother and in some cases a single father.

Generation Z (born: 1995-2012). While we don't know much about Gen Z yet, we know a lot about the environment they are growing up in. Gen Z kids will grow up with a highly sophisticated media and computer environment and will be more Internet savvy and expert than their Gen Y forerunners.

My hope is that the generation X, Y, Z fathers are going to father better than the generations before them. I hope that the trend of seeking to correct the wrongs of previous generations will continue. I just hope that we shall not go from one extreme to another. I hope we can avoid ditch to ditch thinking; an either/or scenario.

Generation Z are growing up with a redefinition of many things, different than they were only 100 years ago. On 26th June, 2015, the Supreme Court in the US legalized gay marriage. What was unthinkable to the depression era generation is a living reality of the generation Y and generation Z. With family redefined by leading socialites, conversations about fathering are bound to become uncomfortable to some, yet the role of fathering cannot be ignored or given a back seat.

Never before have we experienced as many school shootings in world history as we have seen with Generation Y young people. One wonders where all this anger is coming from. This is not a case of terrorists shooting school kids. It is school kids shooting their teachers and fellow kids.

One could blame the increase of these horrific TV stories on the advancement of technology, arguing that CNN, Fox News, BBC and the like are being super efficient in broadcasting these stories. I don't agree.

The New York Times[13] reported that F.B.I released a report confirming a sharp increase in mass shootings in the USA. There were, on average, 16.4 such shootings a year from 2007 to 2013, compared with an average of 6.4 shootings annually from 2000 to 2006. In the past 13 years, 486 people have been killed in such shootings, with 366 of the deaths in the past seven years. In all, the study looked at 160 shootings since 2000 (Shootings tied to domestic violence and gangs were not included). Roughly 45 percent of the shootings occurred in offices or stores, and about 25 per cent at schools or universities. This means that US schools and Universities have witnessed 40 mass shootings on their campuses and, according to F.B.I, these incidents are on the increase.

If this isn't a wakeup call for us to change the trend of bad fathering, I wonder what is. As I have come to learn, the US has a huge influence on most societies in the world. We may not have experienced mass shootings in other nations, but there are many either angry or indifferent generation Y'ers walking around this planet.

There is a desperate need for men who can father this lot, men who are going to risk all in order to father them.

Fathering is a careful combination of cheerleading and coaching, challenging and inviting, celebrating and questioning, building character and tearing down wrong mentalities. The absence of either one of these has led to us having very imbalanced people and, in some cases, very imbalanced generations.

Every generation must be given a good chance at success. They must be given invitation and challenge.

I would like to point you to the heart of God and a valuable lesson for us fathers to learn and remember.

This story has been used to teach and illustrate many lessons for many centuries since Jesus first told it. It speaks of relating to God (likened to the father in the story) based on His love and grace and not our own works of righteousness. There are also many other lenses one could use to see it.

Then He said: "A certain man had two sons. And the younger of them said to his father, 'Father, give me the portion of goods that falls to me.' So he divided to them his livelihood. And not many days after, the younger son gathered all together, journeyed to a far country, and there wasted his possessions with prodigal living.

But when he had spent all, there arose a severe famine in that land, and he began to be in want. Then he went and joined himself to a citizen of that country, and he sent him into his fields to feed swine. And he would gladly have filled his stomach with the pods that the swine ate, and no one gave him anything.

"But when he came to himself, he said, 'How many of my father's hired servants have bread enough and to spare, and I perish with hunger! I will

arise and go to my father, and will say to him, "Father, I have sinned against heaven and before you, and I am no longer worthy to be called your son. Make me like one of your hired servants."'

"And he arose and came to his father. But when he was still a great way off, his father saw him and had compassion, and ran and fell on his neck and kissed him. And the son said to him, 'Father, I have sinned against heaven and in your sight, and am no longer worthy to be called your son.'

"But the father said to his servants, 'Bring out the best robe and put it on him, and put a ring on his hand and sandals on his feet. And bring the fatted calf here and kill it, and let us eat and be merry; for this my son was dead and is alive again; he was lost and is found.' And they began to be merry.

"Now his older son was in the field. And as he came and drew near to the house, he heard music and dancing. So he called one of the servants and asked what these things meant. And he said to him, 'Your brother has come, and because he has received him safe and sound, your father has killed the fatted calf.'

"But he was angry and would not go in. Therefore his father came out and pleaded with him. So he answered and said to his father, 'Lo, these many years I have been serving you; I never transgressed your commandment at any time; and yet you never gave me a young goat, that I might make merry with my friends. But as soon as this son of yours came, who has devoured your livelihood with harlots, you killed the fatted calf for him.'

"And he said to him, 'Son, you are always with me, and all that I have is yours. It was right that we should make merry and be glad, for your brother was dead and is alive again, and was lost and is found.'" (Luke 15:11-32)

In this story, we see a father who first and foremost loved his children enough to let them make decisions and live with the consequences of their decisions. Even when the younger son's request for his inheritance was tantamount to wishing his father were dead (in the context of the culture where this story was told), the father did not object. It must have hurt but he let it be.

Disciplining our children many times requires that we let them face the consequences of their actions especially early on. When our son was still a toddler, he took a liking for candle fire. Every single time that a candle was lit, he stretched his finger out in an attempt to touch the fire. My wife and I kept trying to keep him away from the danger of the fire. We tried so hard to get him to understand how dangerous fire was. He never seemed to pay attention to our pleas.

One day, a few weeks to his first birthday, he was at it again. My wife then decided to let him experience the feeling of a candle fire. He stretched out his first finger, touched the fire, let out a sharp but brief scream and the lesson was over. He got it immediately. He never once did attempt to touch the fire again.

Sometimes, we need to let our children face the consequences of their decisions. When we keep punishing them for any attempts at deciding anything different from our commands, we are literally saying they have no power to make the right decisions. When they grow up, that's exactly how they will behave. They will always play the victim. They will find it difficult to own up to their decisions and take the responsibility for the consequences. Danny Silk expertly deals with this angle of fathering in his book, *Loving our Kids on Purpose.*

An even greater challenge is fathering with meekness. One of my fathers, Chris Komagum, described meekness as "Strength under Control." When our children are born, we wield all the power and have all the strength. The decisions we make for them are final and can either damage their lives for good or give them a bright future.

Life however quickly shows us that totalitarian rule is a very short-lived style of fathering leadership. Soon the children start to question you and your decisions, measuring you up against

your very own behavior and the values that you espouse. Questions of this kind become the order of the day: "Daddy, how is it that you tell us not to leave table before everyone is done eating yet you leave as soon as you are done?"

You quickly realize that shock and awe just won't cut it. You have to reason together with your children if you are to be effective in fathering them. You must reason with them if you are looking to make head way with lifetime lessons and not short-term compliance to avoid your wrath.

Meekness is a virtue of fathering. Keeping your strength and temper in check yields greater dividends than belting out commands in order to subjugate your children.

Men who have failed at meekness have suffered lots of running battles with their teenagers and total defeat when the children finally leave home and never want to see them or talk to them thereafter. To these children, it seems like they have escaped a home that can only be described as a torture chamber.

In this story, the father consented to his younger son's request in order to let him learn from his mistrust of the father's plans for him. Just like God has always allowed us free will, we need to learn to let our children have free will. We need to learn to harness their free will and guide them in choosing right as compared to making them do right. One is long-term with great results while the other is short-lived with terrible results in the long run. When the younger son saw the consequences of his bad decisions, he had a change in mind. He realized that his life was leading nowhere. It is his confidence in his father's ability to take him in that really strikes a chord however. He had confidence that the man he wished dead loved him enough to receive him back. It is love to receive back a greedy murderous son even in the form of a servant. We know however that this father received him back as a son and threw him a party. That is extravagant prodigal love demonstrated right there.

That is invitation and forgiveness of immense proportions. That is the kind of love that you are actually capable of having for your children. The kind of love that makes a father a cheerleader for their children regardless of the lowest of lows they may sink into.

I have seen some fathers walk side by side with their children in their lowest moments.

Recently, I watched a documentary on BBC that showed how Derek Redmond pulled a hamstring at the Barcelona 1992 Olympics men's 400 meters semi-final race. He and all the Brits were shuttered and utterly disappointed. It was his best year, he was one of the favorites to win that race, yet he plummeted when it counted the most.

Then he heard the voice of his father. His father was right there on the race track while he lay down writhing in pain and agonizing about his missed opportunity. His father lifted and supported his grimacing son to just a few meters before the finish line.

By that time the officials were cross at the father. He was deemed to be wasting time yet to his son, he was becoming an unforgettable hero.

In what seemed like forever, Derek finally crossed the finish line, minutes after the last racer had crossed it. He was the last in the race but was not alone. He crossed the line, knowing he had a father who was not ashamed of him even at the lowest moment in his career. Derek Redmond lost his opportunity to win a gold medal but Jim Redmond, his father, walked away that day having won the Gold in Fathering.

We must decide to celebrate our children and be there for them even when we are not proud of their current state. We must learn to see good in them even when all the outward indicators show they are a forgotten cause. We need to be generous with our compliments and our belief in our children. We must hope that good will always come out of them.

The man I know to provide very powerful lessons on invitation when raising children is Uncle Ben.

Uncle Ben has been extremely supportive of his children. He bathed his girls and boys from when they were little. He has been and continues to be a sure listening ear for them through every stage of life.

Despite the fact that every child of his is significantly different from the other, Uncle Ben has supported them and invited them to learn from him even as he cheered them along.

Jackie, his firstborn, is a lawyer and a political and women's rights activist. In a country like Uganda, where we have a very young democracy, a daughter like Jackie is bound to rub some political honchos the wrong way. You would have thought that Uncle Ben would have moved swiftly to silence her voice. Instead, he has quietly supported her cause and let her be. She actually makes some very good points standing against some injustices in our society.

Gloria is a building design enthusiast. I have not been very much in touch with her since she moved from Uganda over a decade ago but I know she has had the support of her father through the years. Her journey got tough at some point but she eventually achieved her dream and has a supportive father to thank.

Rachel is a brilliantly fast thinker. She reads through stacks of pages in an amazingly short period of time. Her brain has been put to good use in the field of journalism. She once joined a master's class at Makerere University and like it is in most master's classes, they were given a reading list. From my recollection, Rachel was topping her class when she discovered that one of her lecturers was dishing out notes that were quoted verbatim from one of the books on the reading list. She summarily left the masters program. The response from her African father, Uncle Ben, was not the typical threats one would expect. It was an understanding of the total frustration that his daughter was experiencing with the education system. Rachel is better off reading on her own. I am sure she is better than many lecturers out there at journalism anyway.

Paulo, to whom I am eternally grateful for inviting me into the Mugarura family, had a natural gifting with computers. He had a great job with the United Nations and was one of the guys among our peers who, in the economic sense, had hit the ground running straight out of university. He suddenly got this strong sense to leave Uganda for his country of birth, Canada. He left all his achievements behind with no solid plan on where to start life in a country he had last lived in as a child.

His reintegration was everything but easy. He worked at a fast food restaurant and did some stints as a worship pastor at some churches. He later married and started a church, Pivot 613 in Ottawa. Through all the tough times that Paulo faced, you will hear him say for sure that Uncle Ben was always there to encourage and support his dreams and vision. Over the years, Uncle Ben and his wife, Aunt Joy, have done North American tours to support their children in whatever endeavors they have embarked on.

Peter, their last born has had a liking for records from when he was little. Under the watchful eye of his father, he played around with the reel-to-reel machine until he made sense of how it works. He was a great sound man in his teenage years and later on evolved into a fully fledged DJ with quite a following in Kenya and Uganda. You may have to ask for DJ Twonjex if you want to find him.

None of Uncle Ben's children will stand up to say, "My father tried to block my pursuit of a dream or idea I had." Uncle Ben is encouragement in flesh and blood.

What he did for his biological children is also what he did for so many of us.

When I bought my first car, a white Corolla SE limited, locally called Kikumi, it was to Uncle Ben's that I drove it first. I wanted him to see it. He was my father and I needed to be celebrated. I also needed him to lead me in thanksgiving for it. He did both with so much gusto.

Uncle Ben allowed numerous young people to walk into St. Francis Chapel in Makerere University, pick whatever musical instrument they desired and bang on it until a sound more pleasant than noise came forth. The chapel administrators were always frustrated with the rate at which the young people spoilt really expensive equipment. They often took the matter to Uncle Ben in his capacity as the Chaplain, hoping he would call time out on the young people's exploration and learning. He often answered with a characteristic, "Hmmm," and that would be it. He was a defender of the resident, untapped talent within young people.

Many of the famous Ugandan gospel music groups from 1980 to 2007 were developed under Uncle Ben's unrelenting invitation and encouragement. Groups like AYF, Heaven Bound, Destiny, Voices of Victory, Dove7, Praise Group, Drama Group, KYAM, Come Alive and Worship Harvest alongside many notable individual musicians can trace their success to Uncle Ben's unwavering invitation of young people to participate in music.

It was not uncommon for Uncle Ben to invite a totally inexperienced youth to preach through three Sunday services to a congregation that had numerous university professors. If you heard them speak initially, you would be certain they were in to their eyebrows. The congregation would often have to suffer through the beginning days of this lot.

Many really good preachers, teachers and prophets of our day will trace their success back to the days that Uncle Ben offered them an opportunity to punch above their weight. These included Reverend Engineer Paul Wasswa, Fred Muhumuza (PhD), Moses Mukisa, Lynnet Kyomugisha Nsubuga, Reverand Steven Shalita and many more.

The other side of fathering requires that we challenge our children to be the best that they can be. It requires that we believe in them strongly enough not to allow them to give up on life and imagine that the whole world is against them. We cannot allow them to think of themselves as perpetual failures who cannot achieve anything in life.

Moses Mukisa, a good friend of mine, once put it this way, "In a bid to show unconditional love to your children, don't give them the deceptive idea that the world revolves around them and they can have whatever they want."

The father in the Prodigal son's story pushed back against his older son's small thinking. He challenged him to see the bigger picture. He challenged him to see that the life of his brother was worth more than the fattened calf or the material stuff that had been squandered.

Albert Einstein said, "The world is a dangerous place to live, not because of the people who are evil, but because of the people who don't do anything about it."

If you do nothing about the wayward ways of your child, your indecision will come back to haunt you some day.

Edmund Burke said, "The only thing necessary for the triumph of evil is for good men to do nothing."

We are increasingly getting generations of youth that cannot take correction because fathers have absconded from their duty of disciplining their children. Many times, this is because fathers have failed in their duty to love.

Zig Ziglar once said, "To a child, Love is spelt T-I-M-E." It is in the abundance of time spent with our children that we shall have opportunity to pass on critical life lessons. Quality time is a product of large quantities of time.

You must learn how to spell and live out love. In our day and age, fathers are up so early to go to work and come back so late, tired, and unable to spend time with their children.

When you spend time with your children, you are able to see their defaults, and because you have loved them with a language they understand (TIME), you have a right into their hearts to call out their wrong as soon as you see it. The children are happy to seek correction because they value being in right standing with you. Relationship trumps rules every single time. That's why T.I.M.E is important. There can't be relationship without time.

The writer of Proverbs in the Bible says;

Train up a child in the way he should go, And when he is old he will not depart from it .(Proverbs 22:6)

He who spares his rod hates his son, But he who loves him disciplines him promptly. (Proverbs 13:24)

In the post millennial times we live in, the use of the rod of correction on children is a divide that has our societies split. The chasm between the proponents and opponents of this method of discipline has never been wider in history than it is today.

Luckily, the argument I am putting across has nothing to do with either.

We can all agree that he is not a responsible father who only challenges his children. Neither is he a responsible father who only cheers on his children and never challenges the wrong things they do.

Foolishness is bound up in the heart of a child; The rod of correction will drive it far from him. (Proverbs 22:15)

Fathering is a balancing act between challenging and cheerleading, invitation and challenge. Our children will feel most loved when we not only celebrate them but also when we caution them or stretch their paradigms. There is Gold in Fathering with Invitation and Challenge.

Chapter Ten: Fathering with Correction

King Solomon, David's son, wrote,
Correct your son, and he will give you rest;
Yes, he will give delight to your soul. (Proverbs 29:11)
I believe Solomon had more reason to say this proverb beyond just being wise. He was a firsthand witness to what happens with a fathering style that is perpetually passive regarding correction of children.

One of the most popular stories in the Bible is David's story. David was a guy. From David, many men have drawn inspiration to overcome hardships and lessons on what to do and what not to do. He was the shepherd boy who killed a lion, a bear and Goliath, a giant from Gath. He was an accomplished soldier and a respected general. He was a keen follower and worshiper of the God of Israel and one of Israel's greatest kings.

The Bible however does not hide his weaknesses inasmuch as it celebrates his strengths. You can be excellent at work, the friendliest guy in the club and a philanthropist like never seen before but fail in your fathering role. That's how simple fathering is. Our complexities cannot explain it away. We are either fathering or we are not.

His many victories, much wisdom and strategic thinking notwithstanding, we see a rather odd picture of David as a father. I do not seek to minimize the achievements of this giant of a man but rather seek to glean some lessons on fatherhood for all fathers to learn, especially concerning correcting our children.

For some reason, David simply avoided confronting any wrong that his children did. He typically avoided correcting them. He always lay low and seemed to hope that matters would auto correct. This war hero had killed a giant but somehow always avoided conflict resolution with his children. Only the avoidable death of his children seemed to put matters to bed.

After this Absalom the son of David had a lovely sister, whose name was Tamar; and Amnon the son of David loved her. Amnon was so distressed over his sister Tamar that he became sick; for she was a virgin. And it was improper for Amnon to do anything to her. (2 Samuel 13:1-2)
A lot more than what meets the eye was going on in David's household.

One wonders what was happening to other young girls who were within close proximity to the king's son. From the onset, it is easy to tell that Amnon was a serial abuser of women. His biggest problem with Tamar was that she was a virgin. It never was because she was a King's daughter.

We know that kings get to know a lot about what is going on in their kingdoms. It is not possible that David did not know about Amnon's clandestine activities. When we let our children's behavior go unchecked, we are unleashing monsters upon the children of others. The bigger the monster grows, the bolder it gets.

But Amnon had a friend whose name was Jonadab the son of Shimeah, David's brother. Now Jonadab was a very crafty man. And he said to him, "Why are you, the king's son, becoming thinner day after day? Will you not tell me?"

Amnon said to him, "I love Tamar, my brother Absalom's sister."

So Jonadab said to him, "Lie down on your bed and pretend to be ill. And when your father comes to see you, say to him, 'Please let my sister Tamar come and give me food, and prepare the food in my sight, that I may see it and eat it from her hand.'" Then Amnon lay down and pretended to be ill; and when the king came to see him, Amnon said to the king, "Please let Tamar my sister come and make a couple of cakes for me in my sight, that I may eat from her hand."

And David sent home to Tamar, saying, "Now go to your brother Amnon's house, and prepare food for him." So Tamar went to her brother Amnon's house; and he was lying down. Then she took flour and kneaded it, made cakes in his sight, and baked the cakes. And she took the pan and placed them out before him, but he refused to eat.

Then Amnon said, "Have everyone go out from me." And they all went out from him. Then Amnon said to Tamar, "Bring the food into the bedroom, that I may eat from your hand." And Tamar took the cakes which she had made, and brought them to Amnon her brother in the bedroom. Now when she had brought them to him to eat, he took hold of her and said to her, "Come, lie with me, my sister."

But she answered him, "No, my brother, do not force me, for no such thing should be done in Israel. Do not do this disgraceful thing! And I, where could I take my shame? And as for you, you would be like one of the fools in Israel. Now therefore, please speak to the king; for he will not withhold me from you." However, he would not heed her voice; and being stronger than she, he forced her and lay with her. (2 Samuel 13:3-14)

If Amnon had no fear of his father's reprimand concerning his own sister, what are the chances that he would have had any regard for any other family in Israel?

David asked his daughter to go attend to her brother Amnon. Even when guised and coated with politeness, it was a king's command. She could not refuse a king's command. She faithfully obeyed, prepared cake for her brother, who raped her in return.

A close look at the conversation between Tamar and Amnon reveals that she was willing to give in to her brother's demands if only he asked the king for her hand in marriage. It is not clear what the boundaries for incest were back then but suffice it to say that she was sure her father would have consented to their union.

Amnon disregarded her pleas and more importantly had total disregard of his father, the king. For some reason, he was sure he could get away with rape. And he did.

Then Amnon hated her exceedingly, so that the hatred with which he hated her was greater than the love with which he had loved her. And Amnon said to her, "Arise, be gone!"

So she said to him, "No, indeed! This evil of sending me away is worse than the other that you did to me." But he would not listen to her.

Then he called his servant who attended him, and said, "Here! Put this woman out, away from me, and bolt the door behind her."

Now she had on a robe of many colors, for the king's virgin daughters wore such apparel. And his servant put her out and bolted the door behind her.

Then Tamar put ashes on her head, and tore her robe of many colors that was on her, and laid her hand on her head and went away crying bitterly. And Absalom her brother said to her, "Has Amnon your brother been with you? But now hold your peace, my sister. He is your brother; do not take this thing to heart."

So Tamar remained desolate in her brother Absalom's house.

But when King David heard of all these things, he was very angry. And Absalom spoke to his brother Amnon neither good nor bad. For Absalom hated Amnon, because he had forced his sister Tamar. (2 Samuel 13:15-22)

Amnon hunted down his ultimate prey and successfully got what he wanted without any caution from his father. His unchecked behavior had come full circle in David's own house. He raped his sister under his father's watch.

What was David's response to Tamar's rape? Anger. And that was it. I certainly would be angry, wouldn't you? I would also do something correctional about it. However, that was never David's response. He fathered his children with a general aversion to correcting them. He never once confronted Amnon. He did not call out his wrong. He did not even try any remedies for his raped daughter.

For two years, Absalom watched as David neither said a word of consolation to Tamar nor did anything to Amnon concerning his shameful rape of his sister.

In my mind's eye, I imagine that these children somehow knew that they were far from the discipline, correction or rebuke of their father.

And it came to pass, after two full years, that Absalom had sheepshearers in Baal Hazor, which is near Ephraim; so Absalom invited all the king's sons. Then Absalom came to the king and said, "Kindly note, your servant has sheepshearers; please, let the king and his servants go with your servant."

But the king said to Absalom, "No, my son, let us not all go now, lest we be a burden to you." Then he urged him, but he would not go; and he blessed him.

Then Absalom said, "If not, please let my brother Amnon go with us." And the king said to him, "Why should he go with you?" But Absalom urged him; so he let Amnon and all the king's sons go with him. (2 Samuel 13:23-27)

Once again, another of the king's sons manipulates the soft spot that David had for his children. He executes his carefully crafted plan with astounding mastery. He starts by inviting his father to his sheep shearing party. The Bible does not tell us whether he knew his father would turn his invitation down or not. What it says is that he pushed hard for his father's attendance and then expertly turned the request into an invitation of Amnon.

The king must have known that there was bad blood brewing between Absalom and Amnon. Let's not forget that Tamar lived at her brother's house from the time of her disgraceful rape. Amnon was going to see his sister for the first time after two full years since the incident. The king sends his son Amnon to Absalom's house with two years of tension well-known to him.

The king knowingly asked Absalom why he wanted Amnon to attend but did not seek any reassurance from Absalom of no foul play. If you were David, wouldn't you have attempted to get some reassurances of no foul play from Absalom? I believe I would. However, I think that if I had also done nothing about Tamar's rape for two full years, I would have no moral authority to caution Absalom. The plot thickened fast.

Now Absalom had commanded his servants, saying, "Watch now, when Amnon's heart is merry with wine, and when I say to you, 'Strike Amnon!' then kill him. Do not be afraid. Have I not commanded you? Be courageous and valiant."

So the servants of Absalom did to Amnon as Absalom had commanded. Then all the king's sons arose, and each one got on his mule and fled.

And it came to pass, while they were on the way, that news came to David, saying, "Absalom has killed all the king's sons, and not one of them is left!" So the king arose and tore his garments and lay on the ground, and all his servants stood by with their clothes torn. Then Jonadab the son of Shimeah, David's brother, answered and said, "Let not my lord suppose they have killed all the young men, the king's sons, for only Amnon is dead. For by the command of Absalom this has been determined from the day that he forced his sister Tamar. Now therefore, let not my lord the king take the thing to his heart, to think that all the king's sons are dead. For only Amnon is dead."

Then Absalom fled. And the young man who was keeping watch lifted his eyes and looked, and there, many people were coming from the road on the hillside behind him. And Jonadab said to the king, "Look, the king's sons are coming; as your servant said, so it is." So it was, as soon as he had finished speaking, that the king's sons indeed came, and they lifted up their voice and wept. Also the king and all his servants wept very bitterly.

But Absalom fled and went to Talmai the son of Ammihud, king of Geshur. And David mourned for his son every day. So Absalom fled and went to Geshur, and was there three years. And King David longed to go to Absalom. For he had been comforted concerning Amnon, because he was dead. (2 Samuel 13:28-39)

Here is the wonder of all wonders. David's daughter is raped and he does nothing. His son is murdered and he does nothing.

NOTHING!

Absalom fled possible wrath from his siblings but as we see later in this story, he didn't flee for fear of his father's wrath or correction. The Bible would have said so if it was the case.

The king wept and mourned his son Amnon. He mourned his son every day. Then after three years, he was over his son Amnon and longed to see Absalom. There was no decree issued against the murder. There was no mention of a word from David that talked down such behavior. He wept and that was it.

I hope that we can father better than this. Fathering is not a competition for being liked by our children. One would hope that being liked is an outcome of great fathering but we cannot sacrifice disciplining our children on the altar of cheap popularity. Here is what the writer of Hebrews says concerning discipline;

And you have forgotten the exhortation which speaks to you as to sons: "My son, do not despise the chastening of the Lord, nor be discouraged when you are rebuked by Him; for whom the Lord loves He chastens, and scourges every son whom He receives."

If you endure chastening, God deals with you as with sons; for what son is there whom a father does not chasten? But if you are without chastening, of which all have become partakers, then you are illegitimate and not sons. Furthermore, we have had human fathers who corrected us, and we paid them respect. Shall we not much more readily be in subjection to the Father of spirits and live? For they indeed for a few days chastened us as seemed best to them, but He for our profit, that we may be partakers of His holiness. Now no chastening seems to be joyful for the present, but painful; nevertheless, afterward it yields the peaceable fruit of righteousness to those who have been trained by it. (Hebrews 12:5-11)

It is important to note that chastening is an expression of love. Sons that are not corrected are considered illegitimate and not sons at all. In other words, it is a demonstration of little or no concern on the part of a father for the child's future.

When fathers correct us, we pay them respect. Respect for you as a father and right living on the part of your children are the natural outcomes of correction even though it is painful at the moment of issuing it.

By the way, David was not passive with all his sons. All but one of David's sons was short changed on his fathering role. He specifically gave time, guidance and correction to Solomon. He raised him up to be king after him. He taught Solomon what the most important treasure for kings was – wisdom and understanding. No wonder when God came asking Solomon for one thing he needed, it was wisdom he requested.

These are the words of Solomon;
Hear, my children, the instruction of a father,
And give attention to know understanding;
For I give you good doctrine:
Do not forsake my law.
When I was my father's son,
Tender and the only one in the sight of my mother,
He also taught me, and said to me:
"Let your heart retain my words;
Keep my commands, and live.
Get wisdom! Get understanding!
Do not forget, nor turn away from the words of my mouth.
Do not forsake her, and she will preserve you;
Love her, and she will keep you.
Wisdom is the principal thing;
Therefore get wisdom.
And in all your getting, get understanding. (Proverbs 4:1-7)

In the midst of a plot with rape, intrigue and murder, you have to applaud David for his gracious nature toward his children. It can only be likened to God's grace toward us all. I strongly believe that without the grace of our Lord Jesus, there is absolutely no way that we can stand before God. There is no relationship without grace and relationship trumps rules every single time.

However, I would like to emphasize that grace comes with responsibility. Those who receive the abundance of grace from God and the gift of righteousness receive them with a responsibility to reign in life (see Romans 5:17). I can tell you that reigning as king is a huge responsibility.

You would imagine that Amnon's murder was the end of David's passive fathering with no correction of his children. I wish it was but that was never to be. One event led to another and Absalom returned to the comforts of being a prominent prince with literally nothing done about his crime. David was literally growing a monster under his roof.

So Joab the son of Zeruiah perceived that the king's heart was concerned about Absalom. And Joab sent to Tekoa and brought from there a wise woman, and said to her, "Please pretend to be a mourner, and put on mourning apparel; do not anoint yourself with oil, but act like a woman who has been mourning a long time for the dead. Go to the king and speak to him in this manner." So Joab put the words in her mouth.

Then she said, "Please let the king remember the Lord your God, and do not permit the avenger of blood to destroy anymore, lest they destroy my son."

And he said, "As the Lord lives, not one hair of your son shall fall to the ground."

Therefore the woman said, "Please, let your maidservant speak another word to my lord the king."

And he said, "Say on."

So the woman said: "Why then have you schemed such a thing against the people of God? For the king speaks this thing as one who is guilty, in that the king does not bring his banished one home again. For we will surely die and become like water spilled on the ground, which cannot be gathered up again. Yet God does not take away a life; but He devises means, so that His banished ones are not expelled from Him."

Then the king answered and said to the woman, "Please do not hide from me anything that I ask you."

And the woman said, "Please, let my lord the king speak."

So the king said, "Is the hand of Joab with you in all this?"

And the woman answered and said, "As you live, my lord the king, no one can turn to the right hand or to the left from anything that my lord the king has spoken. For your servant Joab commanded me, and he put all these words in the mouth of your maidservant. To bring about this change of affairs your servant Joab has done this thing; but my lord is wise, according to the wisdom of the angel of God, to know everything that is in the earth."

And the king said to Joab, "All right, I have granted this thing. Go therefore, bring back the young man Absalom." Then Joab fell to the ground on his face and bowed himself, and thanked the king. And Joab said, "Today your servant knows that I have found favor in your sight, my lord, O king, in that the king has fulfilled the request of his servant." So Joab arose and went to Geshur, and brought Absalom to Jerusalem. And the king said, "Let him return to his own house, but do not let him see my face." So Absalom returned to his own house, but did not see the king's face. (2 Samuel 14:1-3, 11-13, 18-24)

So Absalom is released from his self-imposed exile. For three years, he stayed in a neighboring kingdom for the fear of the avengers of his brother's blood. He did not flee for fear of his father. The law of the avenger was such that if one who sought to avenge the blood of his or her departed one found the murderer, they had a right to slay him or her. This was only not possible if the man slayer took refuge in one of the cities of refuge. Additionally, he had to have murdered the person accidentally. The murder was never to be premeditated and there was never to be any hatred of the murdered person, prior to the murder. (see Joshua 20:1-7)

Absalom's case was different. He had premeditated Amnon's murder. He knew that much and never attempted to run for refuge to Kirjath Arba the city of refuge closest to Jerusalem in Judea. He made off to Geshur, another kingdom.

In this crafty conversation engineered by the king's army commander, the king lifted the charge of the avenger over Absalom. Not because the high priest had died and not because Absalom was not guilty of cold blooded murder. It was because the king had judged in favor of the woman and therefore could judge in favor of Absalom.

That is political genius. The kind we still see in the courts of many of our rulers to this day.

Joab had helped David to find a legal way to return his son Absalom to the kingdom. His longing to see Absalom was close to being satisfied.

In an uncharacteristic turn of events, David asked that Absalom shouldn't be allowed to see his face. However weakly veiled, he had sent a message to Absalom that murdering Amnon was not okay. Good as this gesture may seem, it still fell short of a clear correction or word concerning the murder of Amnon. Could this have been a political move to show outward displeasure with no real intent to speak about what happened?

Aren't there times when we speak words or gesture correction which both our children and we know is just for show?

Our son had been in the habit of manipulating people through tears, cajoling and every tool in his box of tricks. We both knew that if this went on unchecked, it would be a problem for him and for us in the future.

We not only knew this, my wife totally detested it and championed the cautioning of the little boy.

I, on the other hand, felt that although it was not good behavior, it was not a cardinal sin. I inwardly did not see why we made a mountain out of an anthill-sized problem.

So one evening, after repeated warnings, my wife decided she was going to spank our son. She was determined to stump out that vice. Seeing the viciousness in her eyes, I was certain that Lemmy was in for a good beating. Wanting to save him the mother of all spankings for a vice I felt was not really that bad, I offered to spank him; outwardly pretending that I was equally miffed.

What followed was a total let down of my wife and a revelation of the real intensions of my heart. I literally patted his backside a few times and pretended to sternly caution him.

My wife stormed out of the room. It was clear whose side I was on. My son knew that much too. I was sowing the wrong seed. I was communicating to him that though we said it was terrible what he did, we did not really mean it.

It was hard for me to calm my wife down. That one event got me a sabbatical leave from all happy moments in the bedroom for a while.

That's why I can say that I can easily read into David's political posturing. He wanted to see Absalom. And the murder of Amnon was just another of those things that had happened. It was to be glossed over like he did the rape of Tamar.

Now in all Israel there was no one who was praised as much as Absalom for his good looks. From the sole of his foot to the crown of his head there was no blemish in him. And when he cut the hair of his head—at the end of every year he cut it because it was heavy on him—when he cut it, he weighed the hair of his head at two hundred shekels according to the king's standard. To Absalom were born three sons, and one daughter whose name was Tamar. She was a woman of beautiful appearance.

And Absalom dwelt two full years in Jerusalem, but did not see the king's face. Therefore Absalom sent for Joab, to send him to the king, but he would not come to him. And when he sent again the second time, he would not come. So he said to his servants, "See, Joab's field is near mine, and he has barley there; go and set it on fire." And Absalom's servants set the field on fire.

Then Joab arose and came to Absalom's house, and said to him, "Why have your servants set my field on fire?"

And Absalom answered Joab, "Look, I sent to you, saying, 'Come here, so that I may send you to the king, to say, "Why have I come from Geshur? It would be better for me to be there still. Now therefore, let me see the king's face; but if there is iniquity in me, let him execute me."

So Joab went to the king and told him. And when he had called for

Absalom, he came to the king and bowed himself on his face to the ground before the king. Then the king kissed Absalom. (2 Samuel 14:25-33)

The posturing took another two years but it was not David who called it to an end. It was Absalom. He demanded to see the army commander in order to send word to his father. I find the content of his message full of contempt. In the part of Africa where I was raised, there is no way any son could speak to his father this way.

Absalom saw no wrong in his previous actions. In the reality of his absurd world, he went to Geshur for a holiday that was rudely interrupted by his father and the army commander. Now that his holiday was rudely interrupted with no benefit after two years, he would rather go back to his beach life!

He literally threw an adult tantrum and the king played along, inviting him to the palace to see him and capping it all up with kissing him.

That again is notably gracious coming from David. I still want to uphold that grace is the only way we can be made right. It was the only way this could have ended well.

However, do you notice that Absalom's heart was still unchanged? David had not issued any correction. Absalom therefore felt there was nothing wrong with what he had done five years before, after all.

After this it happened that Absalom provided himself with chariots and horses, and fifty men to run before him. Now Absalom would rise early and stand beside the way to the gate.

So it was, whenever anyone who had a lawsuit came to the king for a decision, that Absalom would call to him and say, "What city are you from?" And he would say, "Your servant is from such and such a tribe of Israel." Then Absalom would say to him, "Look, your case is good and right; but there is no deputy of the king to hear you." Moreover Absalom would say, "Oh, that I were made judge in the land, and everyone who has any suit or cause would come to me; then I would give him justice."

And so it was, whenever anyone came near to bow down to him, that he would put out his hand and take him and kiss him. In this manner Absalom acted toward all Israel who came to the king for judgment. So Absalom stole the hearts of the men of Israel.

Now it came to pass after forty years that Absalom said to the king, "Please, let me go to Hebron and pay the vow which I made to the Lord. For your servant took a vow while I dwelt at Geshur in Syria, saying, 'If the Lord indeed brings me back to Jerusalem, then I will serve the Lord.'"

And the king said to him, "Go in peace." So he arose and went to Hebron.

Then Absalom sent spies throughout all the tribes of Israel, saying, "As soon as you hear the sound of the trumpet, then you shall say, 'Absalom reigns in Hebron!'" And with Absalom went two hundred men invited from Jerusalem, and they went along innocently and did not know anything. Then Absalom sent for Ahithophel the Gilonite, David's counselor, from his city—from Giloh—while he offered sacrifices. And the conspiracy grew strong, for the people with Absalom continually increased in number. (2 Samuel 15:1-12)

The monster was growing a second head! From murder, Absalom started plotting treason against his own father.

For societies that have turned disciplining children into a crime punishable by law, I would like to suggest that we take a second look at our decisions and our laws.

For numerous years, Absalom, plotted against his father. He endeared himself to his father's people and discredited his father's judgments at the city gate even before people got a chance to hear from the king.

He even managed to sway Ahithophel, his father's most trusted and best counselor.

When what is wrong goes on unchecked for long, it is considered right. Absalom rebelled against his father's decision to do nothing about Tamar's rape and killed his brother in retaliation. He got away with it so he now sought to get rid of his father all together.

Take a long term view on disciplining your child. Consider it love to your child and a service to society at large. If you have an undisciplined child, that child will be unleashed on an unsuspecting public and will soon be unleashed on you.

Now a messenger came to David, saying, "The hearts of the men of Israel are with Absalom."

So David said to all his servants who were with him at Jerusalem, "Arise, and let us flee, or we shall not escape from Absalom. Make haste to depart, lest he overtake us suddenly and bring disaster upon us, and strike the city with the edge of the sword."

And the king's servants said to the king, "We are your servants, ready to do whatever my lord the king commands." Then the king went out with all his household after him. But the king left ten women, concubines, to keep the house.

And the king went out with all the people after him, and stopped at the outskirts. Then all his servants passed before him; and all the Cherethites, all the Pelethites, and all the Gittites, six hundred men who had followed him from Gath, passed before the king. (2 Samuel 15:13-18)

Then Absalom said to Ahithophel, "Give advice as to what we should do."

And Ahithophel said to Absalom, "Go in to your father's concubines, whom he has left to keep the house; and all Israel will hear that you are abhorred by your father. Then the hands of all who are with you will be strong." So they pitched a tent for Absalom on the top of the house, and Absalom went in to his father's concubines in the sight of all Israel. (2 Samuel 16:20-22)

Absalom's forces had the upper hand and overran Jerusalem. He sent his father running for his life like a common thief. He also had no intention to save his father's life if he had a chance to kill him. He made his intentions clear by sleeping with all his father's ten concubines in the full view of all Israel. Imagine such a spectacle. It all happened on the rooftop of his father's palace. The top tabloids and leading news stations of the day would not have had to pay for this story. It was there for all to see.

It is possible for a little bouncy baby that you dotingly play with to turn guns on you when he or she is older. Passive fathering can deliver such a misfortune.

I implore you fathers, by the mercies of God, please treat your fathering role with the honor it deserves. It is not a waste of time when you skip the drinks with your buddies at the bar in order to spend time with and correct your children. That one action could just as well be your best gift to mankind.

I once heard one of the leading businessmen in Uganda, say that the one thing he regretted was not spending enough time with his children. He told a story about how he had promised his children time with them but was stuck in a board meeting he was chairing. One of his children stormed into the meeting and demanded that his father leaves with him. It was their time with their father and he was not taking any more intrusion.

He asked to be excused from the board meeting and went off to have time with his children.

He is wise enough to realize that relational capital with his children is far more valuable than the financial capital he was growing in the board meeting.

As a father, are you willing to make such a call in view of your fathering role? Do you consider fathering to be of more value than the stuff that keeps you busy all day long?

Now the king had commanded Joab, Abishai, and Ittai, saying, "Deal gently for my sake with the young man Absalom." And all the people heard when the king gave all the captains orders concerning Absalom.

So the people went out into the field of battle against Israel. And the battle was in the woods of Ephraim. The people of Israel were overthrown there before the servants of David, and a great slaughter of twenty thousand took place there that day. For the battle there was scattered over the face of the whole countryside, and the woods devoured more people that day than the sword devoured.

Then Absalom met the servants of David. Absalom rode on a mule. The mule went under the thick boughs of a great terebinth tree, and his head caught in the terebinth; so he was left hanging between heaven and earth. And the mule which was under him went on. Now a certain man saw it and told Joab, and said, "I just saw Absalom hanging in a terebinth tree!"

So Joab said to the man who told him, "You just saw him! And why did you not strike him there to the ground? I would have given you ten shekels of silver and a belt."

But the man said to Joab, "Though I were to receive a thousand shekels of silver in my hand, I would not raise my hand against the king's son. For in our hearing the king commanded you and Abishai and Ittai, saying, 'Beware lest anyone touch the young man Absalom!' Otherwise I would have dealt falsely against my own life. For there is nothing hidden from the king, and you yourself would have set yourself against me."

Then Joab said, "I cannot linger with you." And he took three spears in his hand and thrust them through Absalom's heart, while he was still alive in the midst of the terebinth tree. And ten young men who bore Joab's armor surrounded Absalom, and struck and killed him. Then Joab said to the Cushite, "Go, tell the king what you have seen." So the Cushite bowed himself to Joab and ran.

Just then the Cushite came, and the Cushite said, "There is good news, my lord the king! For the Lord has avenged you this day of all those who rose against you." And the king said to the Cushite, "Is the young man Absalom safe?" So the Cushite answered, "May the enemies of my lord the king, and all who rise against you to do harm, be like that young man!"

Then the king was deeply moved, and went up to the chamber over the gate, and wept. And as he went, he said thus: "O my son Absalom—my son, my son Absalom—if only I had died in your place! O Absalom my son, my son!"

(2 Samuel 18: 5-15, 21, 31-33)

The very son that David tried to protect, the very son whom he restrained from correcting, the very son who sought to take David's life, was murdered by a cold hearted man in the form of Joab, David's army commander.

Even though David had given express instructions not to harm Absalom, Joab had no kind words for any enemy that sought to destabilize his master or the kingdom they had fought so hard to establish.

I wonder what would have been if Absalom had grown up disciplined and corrected. I wonder what would have been if his murder of Amnon was dealt with firmly. I wonder what would have been if David had checked Absalom's posturing at the city gates.

This rebellion had been long in coming. The king could have stopped it years earlier but he chose to be passive about it. He chose not to correct Absalom. In the end, Absalom lost his life prematurely. In the end, the king's concubines were defiled by their son in the viewing of all Israel. In the end, the untamed monster in Absalom had taken yet another life: his own. Yet even after such calamity, the story of David's passive fatherhood was far from over.

Then Adonijah the son of Haggith exalted himself, saying, "I will be king"; and he prepared for himself chariots and horsemen, and fifty men to run before him. (And his father had not rebuked him at any time by saying, "Why have you done so?" He was also very good-looking. His mother had borne him after Absalom.) Then he conferred with Joab the son of Zeruiah and with Abiathar the priest, and they followed and helped Adonijah. But Zadok the priest, Benaiah the son of Jehoiada, Nathan the prophet, Shimei, Rei, and the mighty men who belonged to David were not with Adonijah. (1 Kings 1:5-7)

It is important to note that yet another son of Haggith had risen to assign himself the throne. Adonijah was Absalom's younger brother. He too was not really fathered by David. He too knew about David's weakness toward his children. When he had fifty horsemen ride before him and proclaim his right to the throne, David knew about it but did not rebuke him. He did not correct him.

Let's not be deceived into thinking that King David was too old to influence things in the kingdom. He was well able to speak and his faculties were all functioning well. He still had the same willpower of the warring and all-conquering young David. Unfortunately he still chose the passive fatherhood that came to mark his family life.

If you let your children know that there are some tantrums you will accept and some ill behavior you can tolerate, they will milk the most out of it. David's children were certain that they were untouchables. Treasonable acts that could get anyone killed in the kingdoms of that day were what his sons toyed with in his full view.

As a father, you must make it clear what you look down upon scornfully. You must draw the line and be sure to enforce it.

When our son was younger, he got accustomed to being rocked to sleep. That was until he made six months when we had to train him to get into bed and sleep on his own. Our friend Marcus Kiryowa let us in on a trick, after we had miserably failed in the bedtime training project.

He said, "Talk to the child calmly, and let him know it's time for bed. Put him in bed, tuck him in and walk away. He will cry and scream his head off for an hour or so but do not flinch. After a while, he will sleep."

I imagined my child screaming for that long and it was painful just thinking about it.

Marcus continued, "Do the same thing every day for a week or so. You will notice that the screaming time will reduce every day. Eventually, he will figure it out that you are not going to compromise on bedtime sleep."

We tried this method out. The first day was horrific. We desperately wanted to run to his bed to pick him up and console him. It is what any loving parent would do, right? Wrong. Loving parents discipline their children. So we encouraged ourselves to wait out the first hour.

As sure as Marcus had predicted, the crying stopped and there was silence, first for a minute, then five, then ten, then thirty. We tiptoed to his bedside to find him fast asleep! We were overjoyed. For the first time in months, he had slept without our arms having to ache. Both our children were quite big babies so rocking them to bed was like rocking a boulder for an hour.

The trick worked. We tried it on day two and it worked. It was also easier to execute. First because we had pulled off the first time which was the most difficult. Secondly, Lemuel had a good recollection that he had lost round one. We soldiered on and after a week, our very wise six-month-old baby figured it was pointless to scream about not being rocked to bed.

The following week, he started sleeping almost immediately after we put him to bed. That was my first lesson on disciplining children. It was a simple and effective lesson.

No matter how old your children are, they are going to push the boundaries to see how far they can push you. They will always test your resolve to see whether you really mean what you say. Your consistency is the best weapon to bring to this fight. You must stay true to your word and even subject yourself to it.

Many times when driving around, the kids would yell at each other on top of their lungs in conversation or arguments. This had become one of my most stressful moments with them. I once shouted them down and my forthright daughter confronted me about it the next morning. I realized I had lost that battle so I apologized for yelling at them.

Following a cue from my wife, I tried out a new approach. When they started yelling, I calmly asked them to speak to each other, warning them that they would have to be quiet for a while if they didn't relent. They obviously carried on like nothing happened, then I made the announcement, "Everyone is going to be quiet in the car for ten minutes!"

Their faces froze in shock.

My wife and I postponed our conversation too. The car was quiet! Oh, what sweet relief! Those ten quiet minutes felt like forever for them.

They were amazing because they got our bundles of love to evaluate their behavior. They also communicated that I was not going to let little terrorists run our home and run us out of town.

We still use that ten minute time out although rarely now, because the yelling in the car is rare. Once again, consistency is the magic bullet.

If you are faced with an indiscipline challenge with your child, regardless of how old they are, be consistent on where you know the line to be. Teenagers may ignore you and pretend your line does not matter. Don't believe their outward show. Inwardly, they desire to be in right standing with you. Love them but don't move the line. We all remember our macho teenage years. We really needed the attention of our parents and the freedom of adulthood all at the same time.

Even as an adult now, it still matters where my father's line is. I have never outgrown the need for his approval. I have never had enough of his smile when he is proud of me.

My father is a firm believer in the unity of the extended family. Having spent many years without his hand to guide me on this matter, I really did not care about the extended family. I don't care as much as he does even now, but he has disciplined me into it even as an adult.

He lets me know what is happening with my uncles, aunts, cousins and the family estate. He lets me know when someone is marrying or when another dies. He lets me know who is sick and who got a promotion. And in all these cases, he expects me to be there for the family. He does not flinch. He speaks to me with utmost confidence, knowing that I will be there. The only time I turn down his invitation is when I am out of the country.

He does not make it feel like I am being summoned. He simply has an expectation of me and entertains no excuses when it comes to family. I have learnt to value the extended family in my adulthood.

There is no one beyond discipline. Not even me.

Back to David's fathering story. David appointed Solomon to be king in his place, thereby clearing the confusion that Adonijah's power-play politics had brought to the palace. David

only did something after Nathan the prophet and Bathsheba his wife intervened. Soon after, David died and once again, the unchecked indiscipline and self entitlement of David's children was at play.

Now Adonijah the son of Haggith came to Bathsheba the mother of Solomon. So she said, "Do you come peaceably?"

And he said, "Peaceably." Moreover he said, "I have something to say to you."

And she said, "Say it."

Then he said, "You know that the kingdom was mine, and all Israel had set their expectations on me, that I should reign. However, the kingdom has been turned over, and has become my brother's; for it was his from the Lord. Now I ask one petition of you; do not deny me."

And she said to him, "Say it."

Then he said, "Please speak to King Solomon, for he will not refuse you, that he may give me Abishag the Shunammite as wife."

So Bathsheba said, "Very well, I will speak for you to the king."

Bathsheba therefore went to King Solomon, to speak to him for Adonijah. And the king rose up to meet her and bowed down to her, and sat down on his throne and had a throne set for the king's mother; so she sat at his right hand. Then she said, "I desire one small petition of you; do not refuse me."

And the king said to her, "Ask it, my mother, for I will not refuse you."

So she said, "Let Abishag the Shunammite be given to Adonijah your brother as wife."

And King Solomon answered and said to his mother, "Now why do you ask Abishag the Shunammite for Adonijah? Ask for him the kingdom also— for he is my older brother—for him, and for Abiathar the priest, and for Joab the son of Zeruiah." Then King Solomon swore by the Lord, saying, "May God do so to me, and more also, if Adonijah has not spoken this word against his own life! Now therefore, as the Lord lives, who has confirmed me and set me on the throne of David my father, and who has established a house for me, as He promised, Adonijah shall be put to death today!"

So King Solomon sent by the hand of Benaiah the son of Jehoiada; and he struck him down, and he died.

(1 Kings 2: 13-25)

As life will have it, someone out there will have to discipline your child if you do not do it yourself. What is more likely is they will not use the same gentle approach that you could have used. What could have been a warning from you, can be death meted by one who is not the father of your child.

When Adonijah, Absalom's younger brother attempted to take the throne forcefully, David could have issued a stern warning against that action. That could have corrected the flowery ideas that Adonijah had in his mind.

The Baganda have a saying, "Akuba owuwe, akuba awumba," meaning, "One who is spanking his own child, softens his strike." That is true all over the world. The world will deal harsher with your child's indiscipline. Solomon dealt much

The notoriety of David's passive fathering was not yet done with the damage it had on his family. After yet another attempt on the king's throne (through the veiled request to marry Abishag the Shunammite, who was effectively David's wife), yet another of David's sons had an untimely death, this time overseen by Solomon the new king that sat on David's throne.

Could David his father have saved his life through correction?

Tamar, Amnon, Absalom and Adonijah lost their lives because of a father that refused to call out wrong as wrong. You may be wondering why I placed Tamar on the list of the dead. It was tantamount to death for a woman to be raped. No one looked her way after that in those days. She was no longer considered an object of love. Her misfortune defined her and went before her. Her rape killed her.

I beseech you to be a father that corrects your children, a father that challenges what is wrong, not letting wrong behavior go unchecked. I hope you choose to father better than David did.

Chapter Eleven: Fathering from the Ashes

One Sunny July afternoon in 1987, my cousin Peter and I were playing soccer. We had a one-on-one contest in which the winner would be the person that scores most goals. One of us played goal keeper while another fired a shot toward his makeshift goal and the other returned the favor on the opposite end thereafter.

The game was going well until Peter fired a shot past my reach onto one of the glass louvers of a window near my goal. The sound of the shattering glass brought our fun-filled game to a screeching halt. Both agape, we pondered how to navigate the ramifications of our game.

It seemed to me that there would be no direct repercussions on my part considering I was the goal keeper and Peter the striker who shattered the window. A few hours later, my Uncle, Peter's dad, returned and another cousin, Nakaleya, reported the event even before he had an opportunity to sit down.

Nakaleya was a better reporter than all the staff at BBC and CNN put together. She was efficient at reporting and was ruthless with the truth. We knew all too well that she was going to tell the first person in authority at their first appearance so we had prepared our defense. The strategy was that we would defend Peter and ensure that he does not get a spanking which was a sure thing for anyone who broke a window pane.

To my surprise however, between Nakaleya's assured reporting and Peter's response, I was the villain. It happened so fast that before I got a chance to say my piece, my uncle back handed me with a slap that had my head oscillate against the door next to me with a number of quick reverberations.

I was confused and angry at the same time. Confused that my coming to Peter's rescue was not a helpful idea but more so that I had taken the punishment and he hadn't.

You see, I was older than Peter and most notably I was the known naughty one. If there was trouble in a one mile radius, it most probably would be attributed to me whether I had been involved in it or not. On this occasion, I was very hurt because in my ten year old mind, I was clearly not the villain.

I remember going to a room that I shared with one of my siblings and crying bitterly before God. I prayed to God that we would leave that home.

For some reason, my parents had not been able to afford an independent home for that season so we were sharing a home with my uncle and aunt's family. We lived in the back quarters and as one would imagine, there was always opportunity to have an inferiority complex.

With hind sight, I realize that it was easy for my mother, my siblings and I to read too much into anything that our gracious host family did or said. In all honesty, I am not even sure whether half the things I heard were true or not. What I remember is that I brushed off most of them but somehow could not get past this particular incident.

I do not remember telling anyone else about it in my family. I did not necessarily have many sympathizers anyway. I was the fellow who had notoriously lost two academic years in one day. The jury was out and the verdict was always going to be guilty where I was concerned.

Even though I came through the window incident with only a slap, I believe it could have been worse. That one incident could have culminated into a colossal inter-family fight between our family and our hosts, if I had escalated it to my mother. My mother is not quarrelsome but my sense is that she was at her wit's end when this incident took place.

In the week that followed my slap incident, I overheard my father and mother having a bitter, heated argument. It had something to do with how my father chose to invest a windfall that he had earned. At the time, my father was involved in property brokerage so this money must have come from a good deal.

My mother had advised him to buy land in the Mabira forest reserve and build a house for us. In her view that was enough money to do that.

Suffice it to say that my father acted different. He decided to use the money to plant a plantain garden. Sadly, nothing of the garden survived. The issue my mother had with him was that he had not listened to her but chosen to listen to one of his siblings instead. She said that she had put up with a lot in the marriage but was not willing not to be listened to as his wife over my father listening to her in-laws.

Our house was on fire. It felt like we lived in a house of cards that was aflame. The tension was palpable. There was no communication between my parents. As children, we perceived it was wise to keep two independent conversations between the two of them lest you mentioned the other in conversation and got caught up in the cross fire.

As had become my father's custom, he left that week to stay with my stepmom and sisters. Barely a day had passed when a truck appeared one afternoon and packed us all up. It happened very fast with no explanation. What was clear was that we were leaving.

I do not recall much time for the pleasantries of saying goodbye to our cousins. There was a lot of muted conversation. There were a few unsure waves, shock and an awkward silence that was rudely interrupted by the long cough, which started the truck engine.

My parents had had an on and off marriage for thirteen years. There were times when my father was absent for long stretches then he would reappear. The period between 1984 and 1987 had been a last ditch effort I believe that to patch up their marriage. As children, we were short on the details but were not in oblivion.

It is important for us to know that children keenly follow what goes on between their parents. As adults, we sometimes hope and want to pretend that they don't but they do. They see the daggers, can touch the tension and read through the facades. Many of the times, they see separation and divorce coming from miles away. Some try to intervene while others resign themselves to fate.

In our case, the fire of separation and divorce had engulfed our home. I was a child then and did not know the extent to which this would bite. I did not know about the shame we would have to bare having to explain to teachers and classmates that our parents' marriage had failed. We had no idea how much it would later on hurt when we saw happy families; children playing with their fathers with the approval of their watching mothers' smiles. The parties that suffer the blow of separation and divorce are way more than the two adults that make the decision. There are children too.

As the truck left that compound in Mulago, I had no idea that it would be the last time I would ever live with my father in the same house. I had no idea that it would be the last time I would wake up to his voice or enjoy the comfort of his protection or provision. Unknown to me, circumstances that day demanded that I grow up. At a tender age of ten and my brother at twelve, we had to fast forward our years for we were now the "men of the house." This was a huge challenge, seeing that we never got a chance to consult with our father on fathering for well over fifteen years after that incident.

Our family as we knew it had been burnt to ashes. I knew about the argument that had ensued a few days before but dared not share it with anyone. I partly thought the argument was the cause of our departure yet on the other hand, I thought it was an answer to my teary prayer. So I blamed myself for what happened. I was sure that if I had not prayed for our departure, my parents' separation would not have happened. This really troubled my mind and heart for many years. It is a burden that I carried everywhere I went.

It is a question that puzzled me for almost two decades until one of my other fathers, my father-in-law, Steven Karebi, wisely counseled me to let it go. He admonished that what was between my parents was their business. I guess he saw a young man that struggled with a possibility that he had been the cause of his parents' divorce.

In the 30th chapter of the book of first Samuel, David had just returned from a close shave likelihood of fighting on a side against Saul his King, Jonathan his best friend and the armies of Israel. King Achish of Gath had wanted David and his men to fight alongside the Philistines but the rest of the Philistine princes thought it a bad idea.

David was notorious among the Philistines and famous among the Israelites. The Philistines had heard it sang by the Israelites that Saul slew his thousands and David his ten thousands. With such a reputation, it was a risky venture to have this guy fight alongside them for he could have turned on them. I believe that was the right call. So they sent back David to Ziklag of Gath, where he had been given refuge from Saul's relentless pursuit to kill him.

David and his men travelled the same three day journey back to Ziklag that they had just done. That was six straight days of travel on foot with heavy military equipment. By the time they got to Ziklag they were exhausted but it could have been worse. They could have been forced to spill the blood of their own kindred.

This is what happened:

Now it happened, when David and his men came to Ziklag, on the third day, that the Amalekites had invaded the South and Ziklag, attacked Ziklag and burned it with fire, and had taken captive the women and those who were there, from small to great; they did not kill anyone, but carried them away and went their way. So David and his men came to the city, and there it was, burned with fire; and their wives, their sons, and their daughters had been taken captive.

Then David and the people who were with him lifted up their voices and wept, until they had no more power to weep. And David's two wives, Ahinoam the Jezreelitess, and Abigail the widow of Nabal the Carmelite, had been taken captive. Now David was greatly distressed, for the people spoke of stoning him, because the soul of all the people was grieved, every man for his sons and his daughters. But David strengthened himself in the Lord his God. (1 Samuel 30:1-6)

I believe that David's dilemma was similar to mine. He must have blamed himself for what happened to their families upon their return to Ziklag. It did not help that his very men blamed him and were making plans to stone him to death. They only considered their loss and not his.

But David encouraged himself in the Lord his God.

If you want a game changer in times of distress, you just got one: encourage yourself in the Lord. There is something inherently difficult about trying to psyche one's self out of trouble. I believe some of the self-help books are not very helpful, for they prescribe a silver bullet that cannot kill emotional and psychological pain.

If you are going through a huge loss and are feeling overwhelmed by it, I suggest you find some scriptures and encourage yourself in God's love for you. You may be faced with separation, divorce, the loss of a loved one, financial loss or wild accusations from close friends that you never imagined could turn their back on you. Encourage yourself in God.

Here are some of the words David actually used to encourage himself in God. Try encouraging yourself with these words and see what happens.

Why are you cast down, O my soul?
And why are you disquieted within me?
Hope in God;
For I shall yet praise Him,
The help of my countenance and my God.(Psalm 43:5)

I will lift up my eyes to the hills—
from whence comes my help?
My help comes from the Lord,
Who made heaven and earth.
He will not allow your foot to be moved;
He who keeps you will not slumber.

There is something terribly wrong with a picture where husbands are separated from their wives and fathers are separated from their sons and daughters. As I stated in the introduction of this book, the harrowing statistics concerning fatherless children being prone to poverty, crime, poor academic performance and early pregnancies are there for all of us to see. I believe that it's for reasons like this that David and his men wept bitterly about it until there was no more strength left in them.

David's men were plotting to stone him to death because the soul of every man was grieved, every man for his sons and daughters. The heart of a father bleeds when separated from their children. It is not a pretty sight. To imagine that a marauding army of ruthless men is keeping company with your daughter, wife or son is totally unbearable. Anything is possible, most of it unimaginable: uncouth mannerisms, abuse, rape, etc.

As the moving truck arrived on the evening of our departure and we pulled into the compound of my mother's little house in Najjanakumbi, one of Kampala's suburbs, we were beginning another chapter of our lives. The house had some tenants that we were forced to share it with for a while. They soon left and it all started to feel like what one would imagine to happen to David and his men's families under the captivity of the Amalekites. We had no father in the house.

My mother has always looked much younger than her age. She has most of the time looked like she was my older sister. For much of my teenage and early twenties, many people would struggle to decipher that ours was a mother-son relationship. So it goes without saying that I had the misfortune of having to wade off the most inappropriate of suitors; from the heckling men in the market, to unruly drivers and worse still, fellow students at school.

When my mother dropped me off on my first day in Senior One at Kings College Budo (equivalent to a first day of Grade 7 at a new Boarding school), one of the older boys asked me to get him my sister's postal address so he could write her a love letter. I tried to clarify that he was asking after my mother but he would have none of it. I had to choose between being beaten up by the bully or concede and play along. I chose the beating.

It was during these times that I got to understand how important a father's covering is. I was only a boy and my brother was not much older. There is so much that women are subjected to in most parts of the world. The heckling and passing suggestions were for the most part unbecoming and downright derogatory.

All over the world, women and girls alike are generally seen as sex objects in many societies. What I experienced made me realize that some men somehow think that because another human being has a biological receptacle for a male organ, they can take their liberties galore. Many women are disrespected and treated as less than human on our watch. This shouldn't be so. We need to protect our mothers, sisters and daughters better than we are doing now.

When we do not caution our fellow men's disrespectful behavior toward women, reasoning that the women in question are not related to us, we fail to realize that these same men can at some point chance on our loved ones. I hope that we will not have to wait until it is our wives, mothers, sisters or daughters that fall victim.

Sadly, some of these notions that undermine women, just like it was for slave trade, are even supported in church circles. The arguments that support this uncouth behavior, though veiled in church, are steeped in tradition and scriptures that say, "Eve ate the forbidden fruit first, so women are the problem." "Paul said women should shut up, so women must be kept voiceless." The most abused is "Women should submit to men. Therefore, women should be under men."

I would like to correct that thinking. First of all, the Bible talks about women submitting to their husbands not to any man that walks the planet. There is exclusivity about that submission. More so, that same portion of scripture admonishes us to submit to one another before it puts a little more emphasis on wives submitting to their husbands. It further puts a bigger burden on husbands to love their wives as Christ loved the Church, even to the point of death. (See Ephesians 5:15-29)

Jesus' attitude has never been of one who lords it over others; His is one of serving others. Love is a service.

In a time when the world did not even consider women worth counting, God hinged His only concrete evidence of the virgin birth of Jesus on a woman, Mary, His earthly mother. Joseph had to believe that Jesus was conceived by the Holy Spirit. He did not see it happen. He had to believe an angel's persuasion in a dream. How many dreams do you take seriously?

When Jesus rose from the dead, the first person that saw Him and told the rest of the disciples that He was risen from the dead was a woman, Mary Magdalene, whom Jesus had healed from the torment of seven demons. The first time she went to the tomb and found Jesus' body gone, the boys did not trust her testimony. Peter and John ran all the way to the tomb to check it out for themselves.

Women like Mary supported Jesus a lot, even financially, in His earthly ministry. Jesus' known friends were two women named Martha and Mary and their brother Lazarus. Jesus often retreated to Martha's house where the three lived.

Jesus stopped for women. He stopped for Peter's mother when she had a fever, He stopped for the woman who had been continuously bleeding for twelve years, He stopped for a Samaritan woman who many Jews despised, He defended and protected women who anointed His feet with oil and used their hair and tears to clean them (apparently, this hair-raising feat was done by more than one woman). Jesus valued and still values women. God created man in His image – male and female He created them.

If we are going to believe in the redemptive work of Jesus on the cross, if we are going to believe that God restored mankind to the place where Adam and Eve were before the fall, then we are going to have to believe that God has restored women too to His image and likeness. It is incumbent upon us to respect God's image.

It is pointless to treat our sisters and mothers anything less than how God sees them. Paul wrote, saying, in Christ Jesus we are all one.

There is neither Jew nor Greek, there is neither slave nor free, there is neither male nor female; for you are all one in Christ Jesus. (Galatians 3:28)

Our roles may be different but there are no second class citizens. God invited women to His table as much as He did the men.

Some of us may continue to be steeped in our traditions and the narrow mindedness of male chauvinism because it serves our benefit. But God sees women making a contribution in transforming the earth to make it look like heaven. He counts their contribution and they shall receive a just reward. God acknowledges women's input whether men here on earth acknowledge it or not.

We are lucky to have seen good women leaders in modern times. I hope this helps us see a better way to treat women. We have seen leaders like Mother Theresa and Margaret Thatcher. Every leader has weaknesses but history will tell you that these women were great leaders. We cannot continue to rubbish women because of their anatomy. That is not God's view point and we can do better than that.

I wish I had an opportunity to say this to most of the men that disrespected my mother in my full viewing. Unfortunate for me, I have always been a small framed person with no muscle mass to boast about. If I had the body of Mr. Universe, maybe, just maybe, I would have attempted to prove my point with might.

The presence and protection of fathers cannot be underestimated. While at my mother's house in Najjanankubi, we were robbed eleven times in nine years, between 1987 and 1996, when my mother sold her house.

It seemed like the robbers waited for my mother to work hard to replace the stolen things before they devised plans to force their way into our house to rob us again. This happened every year. Twice though, the robbers grew impatient and robbed us twice in one year.

Even though it is not unheard of for families to be robbed when a father is present, I can tell you that it is not considered a walk in the park when a man resides in a home. A household headed by a woman seems to be much more vulnerable and susceptible to attacks. Once when the thugs broke in, they ganged up on my older brother because he was the oldest male.

They got all the clothes and books in the house and piled them on him while he lay in bed. One of them, wielding an iron bar, stood between my brother's and my bed. When we tried moving a muscle, he hit us on the head as a warning of what could happen to us if we attempted any rescue mission. We had heard about people who had been murdered in cold blood by these iron bar wielding thugs.

In the meantime, one of them tried to rape our mother in our full hearing. Our little sisters scampered for dear life and hid under a bed that they shared. I heard my mum plead to be spared that embarrassment. She called on the name of Jesus repetitively. We joined in chorus and for some reason, these thugs ran off without harming us.

Not only did we miss the presence and protection of a father, we also did not have any spiritual cover. Allow me delve a little into this matter from an angle that may be different from how you see things.

It is clear from the examples of good fathers in the Bible, that spiritual cover is a man's responsibility. In a portion of scripture that is rarely quoted in this respect, I see Jairus providing cover for his sick daughter.

And behold, there came a man named Jairus, and he was a ruler of the synagogue. And he fell down at Jesus' feet and begged Him to come to his house, for he had an only daughter about twelve years of age, and she was dying.

Someone came from the ruler of the synagogue's house, saying to him, "Your daughter is dead. Do not trouble the Teacher."

But when Jesus heard it, He answered him, saying, "Do not be afraid; only believe, and she will be made well." When He came into the house, He permitted no one to go in except Peter, James, and John, and the father and mother of the girl. Now all wept and mourned for her; but He said, "Do not weep; she is not dead, but sleeping." And they ridiculed Him, knowing that she was dead.

But He put them all outside, took her by the hand and called, saying, "Little girl, arise." Then her spirit returned, and she arose immediately. And He commanded that she be given something to eat. And her parents were astonished, but He charged them to tell no one what had happened.

(Luke 8:41, 42, 49-56)

Jairus knew that Jesus could heal his daughter so he sought His help. He sought to cover his daughter and have her healed. Even when the girl died, Jairus was strengthened by Jesus' assurances and the girl was raised back to life. Jesus only spoke the word.

The man who brought his epileptic son to Jesus' disciples to pray over him for healing was exercising spiritual cover for his son. There is also the Roman centurion who provided spiritual cover for his servant; even the servants in a home are covered spiritually by a father.

Men have a priestly role to play in a home. They cannot fault the spiritual climate in their homes and the outcomes thereof on their wives or the government.

The Bible implores men to train their children. From Abraham's story of the near real sacrifice of Isaac, we see that it was normal for men to engage in matters to do with God with their children. In the book of Acts, there was a man called Phillip who was an evangelist. What makes him stand out is he was known for having four daughters who prophesied. You can be sure that was no mistake. He must have trained his daughters in the things of God. If one daughter prophesied, one could call that chance or luck. Four daughters prophesying speak of this man's intent. (See Acts 21: 8-9)

Here is the dilemma we had when growing up: we had a father who was not present. We had no spiritual cover. I know that you may not consider yourself a very spiritual person but I can tell you that even when you speak positively over your children as a father, you are exercising positive spiritual authority. It is the reason why many people who accomplish great things in life always have a significant authority voice that they quote through their journey to the top.

With the absence of the spiritual cover of a father, we were soon exposed to weird happenings. It was not uncommon for my siblings or me to wake up to a struggle for life, gasping to breathe while no one was physically strangling us. It was not uncommon to wake up to strange smells in the room after experiencing a nightmare.

I remember that as soon as I could, I would shout for help, calling for my mother to come to our rescue. She must have had countless sleepless nights in that time. I remember her instructing us to call on the name of Jesus for help. We did that for a bit with minimal success until she figured that we must learn how to use the authority we had as believers in Jesus to cast out demons and put Satan in his rightful place, underneath our feet.

Her lessons were short and sharp. Having had enough of the torment, our learning followed suit, it was quick and precise. Soon we were able to deal with those situations quite easily all by ourselves. In the months that followed, our confidence actually grew quite a lot in the power and authority of Jesus over the devil.

I know that this part of my story sounds every bit like a script taken out of a Nollywood movie. I can tell you that this was our experience. The difference between our experience and the Nollywood movies is that in real life, believers in Jesus actually cast out demons. In real life, it is the devil that needs deliverance from the believer and not the other way round. In real life we are raised with Christ and are seated in a position of authority far above every power, dominion or principality as Paul reminds us in the book of Ephesians.

Just over our fence, we had a voodoo worship shrine not more than 8 meters from our house. Our neighbor was a known witch doctor and we often saw many come to consult him, both rich and poor. We heard the noises in the shrines; we saw the animal sacrifices, the people in torment being beaten and given herbs. I vaguely recall even one of his patients dying (though that was quickly covered up and no one could tell soon after).

So after many years of chicken and goat heads being thrown over our fence, noises that interrupted our sleep, waking up from nightmares and contending with demons, my brother and I decided we had had enough. What additionally gave us a steel strength resolve was a suspicion we had that the many robberies we experienced had been engineered by Kalyango, the witch doctor's assistant, who also happened to be the secretary for defense on the village. We suspected that the man elected by the villagers to protect us all actually mobilized the thugs who annually came to terrorize us. We were sick and tired of being pushed into the corner. It was our time to push back.

I must have been thirteen and my brother fifteen years old, when this huge celebration of Lubaale Mukasa, one of the demi gods of the Baganda, was meant to begin. People gathered over the fence and a white goat was readied for the slaughter. My brother and I calmly but decidedly declared in Jesus' name that the evil spirits would not manifest as desired by the crowd gathered over our fence. We then carried on playing a game we were engaged in.

Numerous efforts were made to call on the spirits to manifest in the shrine. We could hear what was going on and we knew what it sounded like when they did.

Nothing happened!

One can only imagine our joy. We had declared something and it had happened. The weeklong festival went on with no success and a few months after that, the shrine was moved. Praise God!

It is because of stories like these that we call our mother Mafaza, an endearment which marries the word Mother and Father. We were lucky to have had a mother who filled in the shoes of a father, providing spiritual cover and teaching us as young boys to do the same.

As a father now, I find myself teaching our children from the word of God many nights before they sleep. I have taught them about a believer's authority, the love of God, the Grace of God and many other spiritual truths. I pray over them and bless them literally every night before they sleep. I tell them I love them. I tell them that I am proud of them. I celebrate them, I encourage them and challenge them to learn from me and become better than me. I learnt that from the ashes of not having a father to cover me. I learnt to be that father that I never had.

Whenever my siblings and I turned 12, our Mafaza would have a no-holds-barred conversation with us. It was a show-all and tell-all conversation. She would tell you more than you ever wanted to know about your body and how it worked. She told us about pubic hair growth and other body changes in considerable time before we hit puberty.

I must say that being told about what would happen and experiencing these realities are two different animals. I believe that being a woman, our mother did not know about some significant details like wet dreams, the ever faithful morning erections and others.

I remember once going to her, rather bothered by someone's unkindness to me while I was little. I wanted to know who had slit the bottom of my penis open and stitched it back. I was very convinced of this. The stitch marks were clear even to a partially blind man to see. I showed the 'scar' to my mother and demanded for answers. Although it was rather embarrassing showing her my 'scar', I had to get to the bottom of the matter. I had no father to show it to; I only had a Mafaza.

She took a moment to catch her breath after my shocking accusations. Then she responded matter-of-fact as she always did.

"Chris, when a baby is being formed in their mother's womb, it is two halves that are stuck together."

I looked at her disbelievingly and she followed that up with her classic demonstrations that floor any counter argument.

"Show me both your palms," she said.

I complied, and then she got me to realize for the first time that the patterns of one palm were not exactly identical to the other. For the first time, I got to learn that even one half of a person's face is not the same as the other. I was thoroughly convinced thereafter and have no recollection of bringing up my false allegations again.

What I keep wondering about is; what would my father have said? How would he have navigated those murky waters and what lessons could he have passed on to me? I have never talked about sex or relationships with my father. My father did not offer me any marriage counsel before my wedding. I guess it would have been awkward after not having had these conversations when I was much younger.

As I have shared my story I hope it is clear to you that I do not fault my father at all.

I just hope that my story will jolt an estranged father into action especially when he still has it in his power to make up with his wife and take his place as a father, especially for the sake of his children. I can tell you that the substitutes of fathering are just that: substitutes. No one will ever be a father to your children like you. Only you can father your children the way they ought to be fathered.

I believe that it was for the avoidance of scenarios like what we experienced that David and his men wept for their sons and daughters. You do not want this happening to your children.

Then David said to Abiathar the priest, Ahimelech's son, "Please bring the ephod here to me." And Abiathar brought the ephod to David. So David inquired of the Lord, saying, "Shall I pursue this troop? Shall I overtake them?"

And He answered him, "Pursue, for you shall surely overtake them and without fail recover all."

So David went, he and the six hundred men who were with him, and came to the Brook Besor, where those stayed who were left behind. But David pursued, he and four hundred men; for two hundred stayed behind, who were so weary that they could not cross the Brook Besor. (1 Samuel 20:7-10)

David was a very unique character. Having found his city burnt to ashes and his wives and children taken, having wept to a point of no strength with his men, having had a mutiny brewing a few meters away from him, David had the nerve to ask God whether or not he should pursue the Amalekites to rescue their families.

Are you kidding me? What could be a more obvious course of action?

David still wanted to know what God's will was in this situation and I think we have a lesson to learn here. Even when our course of action seems most obvious, it is important for us to stop and double check with Father God in prayer.

I know that for a man, prayer can look weak to others especially when he decides to pray in circumstances like these instead of kicking into action. From David, we learn that it is better to slowly move forward with God's wisdom than with the speedy ways of man's foolishness.

Many times, it helps to turn to scripture for guidance in difficult times as compared to going with conventional wisdom. This is especially true when you are not sure what to do. If you are honest, many times you won't know what to do. Seeking God's help in prayer does not make you weaker; it makes you stronger. If it worked for King David, one of Israel's greatest kings, it will work for you too.

Prayer helps us to tap into the resources of our heavenly father. We were never made to completely break away from our fathers, whether they are our earthly fathers or our heavenly father. Fathers always have an inheritance for their children, more so God our heavenly father.

You may be separated from your children. Your wife could have sprung a surprise on you and dumped divorce papers on your lap for you to sign. It could be the painful experience of an estranged child. Whatever challenge of fathering you are going through right now. I want you to know that God has answers for you.

As it later turned out, I discovered when I was much older that my father made two attempts to gain access to us after our departure but my mother told him in no uncertain terms that that was never to be. Having grown older, my guess is that access to us could have meant access to her and she was having none of that.

The knowledge of my father's efforts to regain a connection with us has probably been one of the most redemptive pieces of information that I received. For more than a decade, I believed that he never made any attempt. I believed he did not put up any fight for his right to father us. I grew up under the illusion that my father did not like us, that we didn't matter to him. I felt rejected by my very own father.

However late the information came, it warmed my heart to know that I was loved and treasured by my father.

So for David, having got an assurance of God's covering and victory, he pursued the Amalekites with gusto. He was certain to overtake them and redeem all their families and their property.

David however had a matter on his hands. After a six-day walk, his troops were tired. When they got to the brook Besor, two hundred of this army of six hundred could not go further. They were too weary to fight. Two hundred men could not muster the strength to go forward and fight for their families.

I know this to be the situation for some men across the globe. You have got to that place where you have had to call time out on the struggle. You gave it your best shot but your best was not good enough.

Like my father, you came to the realization that you could not move another finger in an effort to redeem your family. I want you to be encouraged that God knows that you gave it your best shot.

You may be feeling like you worked really hard but somehow failed to collect enough wealth to provide for your family. You may be feeling terrible because you have nothing of an inheritance to leave your children or grandchildren.

Maybe you have done time in prison and feel tainted. Your wife and children are not keen to be associated with your name. They do not want to be seen with you in public. You are an embarrassment they'd rather firmly keep shut in the backyard of your home.

Maybe all was going well until you got an ailment that incapacitated you. You can no longer look after yourself as you could before. You need the help of another to take you to the bathroom, to clean you up, or to seat up.

I have seen men in these situations and watched as they have slowly given up on life. I have seen life slowly ooze out of them. A man who has lost the will to soldier on in life can have his life taken by anything. Here is how Solomon stated it in one of his proverbs:

The spirit of a man will sustain him in sickness, But who can bear a broken spirit? (Proverbs 18:14)

Do not give up on yourself. Don't give up the fight. You are not a lost cause. Do not give up hope. Like Shaka Ssali, a famous television host with Voice of Africa, likes to say, "Keep hope alive."

Hope is the only commodity that will keep you around long enough to see your aspirations come to fruition.

Hope deferred makes the heart sick, But when the desire comes, it is a tree of life. (Proverbs 13:12)

Refuse to give up. Your heart's desire will be fulfilled. Your children will be restored to you. Your efforts will amount to something. No matter what the state of your body may be, you are still irreplaceable as a father. Your wisdom still weighs heavier than gold. Your experiences from the life of hard knocks can still save the next generation the pain you went through. Get that spark back into your eyes. You still have lots to offer.

Then they found an Egyptian in the field, and brought him to David; and they gave him bread and he ate, and they let him drink water. And they gave him a piece of a cake of figs and two clusters of raisins. So when he had eaten, his strength came back to him; for he had eaten no bread nor drunk water for three days and three nights. Then David said to him, "To whom do you belong, and where are you from?"

And he said, "I am a young man from Egypt, servant of an Amalekite; and my master left me behind, because three days ago I fell sick. We made an invasion of the southern area of the Cherethites, in the territory which belongs to Judah, and of the southern area of Caleb; and we burned Ziklag with fire."

And David said to him, "Can you take me down to this troop?"

So he said, "Swear to me by God that you will neither kill me nor deliver me into the hands of my master, and I will take you down to this troop." (1 Samuel 30:11-15)

Just like it was for David, sometimes, at the turn of the corner, just when we have decided to slog it out once more, we get a glimmer of hope. We get an idea, someone or a situation offering unexpected help. In David's wildest dreams, he never considered finding this Egyptian who had been left for dead.

Sometimes, out of the seemingly dead situations, life springs forth to our surprise.

Armed with the hormones of youth and the inquisitiveness of my mind, I got through my adolescence like a duck taking a swim. On the surface, it looked like I had it all under control while the turmoil on the inside was every bit like the frantic paddling below the surface of the water. I looked like I had all the answers yet I had more questions within. I looked brave, yet I was quite cowardly on the inside.

When I was fifteen, I used to visit an aunt of mine. Her boyfriend had a daughter my age who stayed at their house. One day when I had gone visiting, I found this girl at their home alone. The girl went into their room and came back to the sitting room with a VHS tape to play a movie. Given the levels of poverty that we experienced, we did not have a TV and I had gone to watch some TV.

By reason of my lack of enough TV time, I did not have much self control when it came to TV. So I was up for whatever was available to watch. She started playing the movie. I clearly remember the title of the movie. It was an innocent girl's name. What followed however got me flabbergasted. The whole movie was sex scenes that did not end. It was the first time I ever watched anything pornographic.

In the meantime, this girl fidgeted around me and I, being absolutely naïve concerning the matters we were watching, I didn't move an inch. It was toward the end of the movie that I figured out what the girl was up to but almost immediately, I heard the voice of Mafaza.

She had always given us all the options in life and then capped it all with this famous statement, "I trust you to do the right thing". So despite all that was going on around me, the voice of Mafaza was loud and clear. I dared not disappoint her. For some reason, she always knew what was going on with us even without telling her about it.

So right there, in that sitting room, with the opportunity to try out sex presented to me, I said no. That was a victory that kept growing my muscle in this area. I have been in very many weird situations since then, staying in various hotels in foreign countries because of work meetings but never giving in to that proposal regardless of the color and shape it took. This experience also taught me that I could decide against the flow.

It is this ability to decide against the flow that helped me to make a decision to love my father as well as my mother. Previously, it had seemed like loving both was dealing treacherously with either one of them. I remember making the decision to love them both and making it clear to them. That's a counter flow decision I made over fifteen years ago.

The TV watching however carried on long after the initial incident. I once again went to watch TV and this one time I set off at one O'clock in the morning to leave for home. Our home was down the hill about two kilometers away.

Our mother tried her best not to have an egotistic fight with us in our teenage years. Like I said earlier, she took on what I think to be a rather more helpful approach, which was, present all the information on what the world looks like, teach us how to make the right choices and express trust in our ability to make the right decisions.

So here I was, walking down the hill at one O'clock in the morning. Anything could have happened to a lanky boy walking alone at that time of the night in the Uganda of that time: getting robbed or mugged, being attacked by wild dogs, or being arrested by security operatives on tramped up charges of being idle and disorderly.

I knew I had overstepped my liberties. I hoped to God that nothing wrong would happen. I was two blocks away from our home when I came face to face with a hyena. This was not a big dog with a weird tail. It was a hyena!

Our eyes locked and I froze. I could not take another step forward.

My very rich imagination immediately went wild with all sorts of imaginations. In those days, it was said that there was a leopard in Kabowa, a village much lower, down the hill. The little scientific facts which I knew were not very helpful at that point. Hyenas usually follow man-eating animals like lions or leopards and pounce on the carcass after the lion or leopard was done sucking blood and eating some flesh.

I had prayed before, but never with as much urgency as I did at that moment. I desperately hoped this was a lone hyena and that there was no leopard in the vicinity. At some point my legs decided to carry me forward. On one hand, I did not want to run for the wild animals can tell when one is in flight mode. Yet on the other hand, I wanted to run as fast as my legs could carry me.

My heart was pounding faster than a motor when I knocked at the door. My mother would at these times be awake praying for our safe return.

My mother, usually quick respond to the door, was taking forever this time. I kept looking over my shoulders, hoping the hyena and the leopard had not surrounded me, ready to pounce.

Then the door opened. I leapt into the house to the amazement of my mother.

She asked me what was wrong and, like every youth trying to prove a point, I said, "Nothing."

It took many months before I attempted returning home late. I had made the wrong choice and it could have been fatal.

However absurd this experience, it gave me an early warning on the consequences of the choices that I made. I learnt to weigh through my decisions. I have not always made the best decisions since but I can tell you that I made much better decisions after my hyena incident.

This lesson came in handy when faced with a choice to be joined with my father or not. Weighing through the options left me with no choice better than being reunited with him.

And when he had brought him down, there they were, spread out over all the land, eating and drinking and dancing, because of all the great spoil which they had taken from the land of the Philistines and from the land of Judah. Then David attacked them from twilight until the evening of the next day. Not a man of them escaped, except four hundred young men who rode on camels and fled. So David recovered all that the Amalekites had carried away, and David rescued his two wives. And nothing of theirs was lacking, either small or great, sons or daughters, spoil or anything which they had taken from them; David recovered all. Then David took all the flocks and herds they had driven before those other livestock, and said, "This is David's spoil." (1 Samuel 30:16-20)

There comes a time in every man's life when you have to fight the battle of your life. When it is your wife, son or daughter involved, the stakes are raised even much higher. All bets are on the table in a winner takes it all fight.

I saw my father press in to win us back to himself exactly fifteen years after we left home. My brother Ronnie was getting married in July of 2002 and he was going to be the first of my mother's children to get married.

My father mobilized most of my cousins, uncles and aunts to rally around my brother to support his traditional wedding (we call it 'Kwanjula') and part of his church wedding. My dad's extended family covered a number of the costs of Ronnie's Kwanjula. That was a bold statement. Love must be relevant. My father's love for my brother and, inadvertently, for us, in this one action, was very relevant and tangible.

After fifteen years of doubts and second guessing my father, it was clear that he loved us. My father was in the thick of things concerning my brother's wedding. That sounded more like news headlines as far as we were concerned although we hoped it was going to last more than that season and it did.

Two years later at my wedding, he was even more involved. I know that my father gave the whole of himself in this season of our lives.

From that point on, I was won over. I was convinced that my father really loved us.

Now David came to the two hundred men who had been so weary that they could not follow David, whom they also had made to stay at the Brook Besor. So they went out to meet David and to meet the people who were with him. And when David came near the people, he greeted them. Then all the wicked and worthless men of those who went with David answered and said, "Because they did not go with us, we will not give them any of the spoil that we have recovered, except for every man's wife and children, that they may lead them away and depart."

But David said, "My brethren, you shall not do so with what the Lord has given us, who has preserved us and delivered into our hand the troop that came against us. For who will heed you in this matter? But as his part is who goes down to the battle, so shall his part be who stays by the supplies; they shall share alike." So it was, from that day forward; he made it a statute and an ordinance for Israel to this day. (1 Samuel 30:21-25)

David made a statute and an ordinance in Israel in which it was established that he who goes down in battle will share the same amount of the spoils as one who stays by the supplies. He literally was saying those who have tussled it out and won are worth the same appreciation as those who genuinely tried and failed at some point.

As we soldier on in the journey of fathering, we shall all get the same spoils, the same rewards. It does not matter whether we botched it along the way. It does not matter whether we are late bloomers and are coming into the game quite late. It does not matter whether we are going through awkward moments of trying to bond with our forty-year-old children.

No matter where you are, if you are committed to fathering, you will have the reward of a father. You will be appreciated by your children.

On 24th July, 2004, I gave a glowing appreciation to my father on my wedding day. I was certain of his love. I was certain that he cared for us, fought for us, sought to protect us the best way he knew how.

It however had not always been the same way in the fifteen years between 1987 and 2002. For some reason, all the painful incidents I described earlier had made me hate my father. The unsolicited attention my mother received, the struggles with voodoo men and the numerous robberies all made me hate him.

I cannot tell you the day this started. What I can tell you is that I loathed him. Even when I occasionally went to his office, to seek for help to pay my school fees, in times when my mother was not in position to, I was seething with anger within, even as I smiled.

I faulted him for not being there. I faulted him for rejecting us. I faulted him for not being able to teach me and show me the way to follow in the trying adolescent years. I faulted him for everything that went wrong.

My anger and bitterness toward him had started much earlier in 1988. He made an effort to look me up at Buganda Road Primary school on a number of occasions. He was looking for Chris Mugga, his son but was told that the boy with that name did not exist. He later on presented all my names at which point the teachers said they knew about a boy called Chris Davis Nsubuga not Chris Mugga. When he demanded to see that boy, it turned out to be me, his son. I hated him so much that I had stopped using our family name. I did not want anything to do with my father. I now go by Nsubuga-Mugga. I use the hyphen to remind me of the reconciliation.

In my bitterness, I also had this fight within me to prove to my father that I was not stupid. To me, he was an opponent, not a father. When he came to school to see me in 1990 just before I did my primary leaving examinations, I asked him what he was doing at my school. I was angry, bitter and full of hatred. In my mind I was the victim of a careless, uncaring, unloving, child-rejecting father. I had built this case against him. Not even the best lawyers in the world could save him from a guilty verdict as far as I was concerned.

When I joined King's College Budo, none of my friends were aware that I had a father. Many of them thought me to be an unfortunate orphan.

A few days to sitting for my Senior Four Examinations, I was asked to go to the headmaster's office. The student who made the announcement said that my father had come to see me. My best friends were shocked. No one thought I had a father. In four years, with the most intimate of conversations, never once had I mentioned my father or anything to do with a father.

He came to see me with an uncle of mine who I really liked. He was the one after whom I was named Chris Nsubuga. My uncle had just returned from Egypt and had bought me a red 'legeza' shirt. They both carried me a card wishing me success in my exams. I received the gift from my uncle and seethed with more anger toward my father.

I wish I could tell you that I got over it sooner. I wish I could tell you that it was a teenage tantrum. It wasn't. I hated my father and anything to do with him for a long time. I privately vowed never to do anything he did. I wanted to be the most far removed of all people from him. It is in hindsight that I can say that was foolishness on steroids. It is amazing how one can be so foolish and still breathe.

I not only had hatred for my father in my heart but also succeeded in detesting two other men in the same vein, along the way. These two were the top bosses of a startup venture that I was involved in. They succeeded in paying us only Fifty thousand Uganda shillings (an equivalent of fourteen US Dollars) per month for hard labor that would sometimes get us to start work at 5am. I thought these two to be the world's most manipulative exploiters. They were scoundrels.

I had a girlfriend then who for some reason really fancied having a leather skirt. A leather skirt cost precisely what my monthly salary was. There was no way I could afford a leather skirt after my meals and transport costs for a month. Honestly I wonder how I lived through those days. The girl dumped me. I kept on joking that it was because I could not afford the leather skirt. It must have been over more serious matters.

One afternoon in 2000, while I has heading out for lunch, I had a conversation with God. He asked me to forgive my father and these two men of their past wrongs, their current wrong doing and any wrong they could do in the future. After a little hesitation, I consented. It is amazing how relieved I was soon after that.

It felt like a heavy stone had rolled off my chest. I had forgiven and had nothing against these men and more so nothing against my father.

By God's grace, I overcame my biggest battle in life. I moved from hatred to love. I moved from seeing the wrongs of my father to seeing his strengths. I moved from reading ill intention in everything he did to reading good motive. My father is a very loving and generous man. He is also a gentleman who does not force his way. Has he made mistakes in life? Yes of course he has. Is he a man I am grateful to be my father? Yes, with all my heart.

My father is very generous; he gives of his time, talent and treasure to anyone who needs it. He is always seeking to help. He is generous with advice. He is an amazing teacher and a great salesman. These are some of the strengths that mark my life. All along, I had no clue that I had learnt them from my father. I had limited time with him in the years that shaped my thinking but I still had time enough to learn the best from him.

Am I as good as he is? I do not know. I hope I am. I can only know if he says that much.

No matter how ugly or convoluted your background may be, you have some good in your heritage. Your father could be dead to you or dead in real life but there is still good in the man that is your father.

If you are hurting and have no relationship with your father, I would like to suggest that it is possible to move from hatred to love. It is possible to come from loathsome thoughts to fond ones. It is possible if you let God help you. It is possible if you forgive as much as God in Christ has forgiven you. It is possible if you forgive like God: past, present and future wrongs. Where forgiveness is, there is evidence of love. That love is deep and has always been there. Forgiveness helps you to see it.

If yours is a story of an offended father, forgive your son or daughter. There is no point in leaving a heritage of pain. There is no point in you dying with your parental blessing. There is no point in your children never exceeding you. Bill Johnson says, "The ceiling of our generation should be the floor of the next generation". Choose to forgive, choose to bless, and choose to catapult the next generation to much greater heights than you scaled. Choose to father.

Out of your lineage could be the greatest human being that will grace the next generations. Out of you could be a Mandela, a Martin Luther King Jr, a Mohamed Ali, a Usain Bolt, a Mother Teresa or a Princess Diana.

Now when David came to Ziklag, he sent some of the spoil to the elders of Judah, to his friends, saying, "Here is a present for you from the spoil of the enemies of the Lord" (1 Samuel 30:26)

Finally, from David we see that our successes are not solely due to our effort. There were elders and friends of his in Judah with whom he shared his spoil. There were people through whose territory David and his men were accustomed to rove; people who caused him to succeed. Such people are worth celebrating whether they are still alive or not.

I will do that for a moment. I want to take off time to honor and thank the men and women who made it possible for my father to be the father he is to me. Mr. Sengendo, his best man, Uncle Matt Mukasa (RIP), Uncle Nambago (RIP), Mr Lwembawo, Mr. Kizito, Mr. Semweya (RIP), Uncle Isaac Matovu (RIP), Mrs. Betty Matovu, Aunt Kenchi (RIP), Uncle Ben Sebalamu (RIP), Uncle Katwere Angel (RIP), Uncle Fred Kiwanuka (RIP) Mr. Chris Nsubuga (RIP), Uncle Dan Kizito, my Grandfather Joseph Makensa Basazzemagya (RIP), his wife Jajja Nkyaye (RIP) and numerous others that I can not mention on these pages. Thank you for all the sobering and encouraging conversations that you had with my father. Thank you for encouraging him not to give up on us. Thank you for supporting us and identifying with us the times when we were with you. Your efforts did not go unnoticed. Your love will be passed down to many generations.

You also have a list of unsung heroes that have made your fathering experience worth the salt. They could have helped you, your father or your grandfather. Please take a moment to jot down those names. Make an effort to thank them or their surviving family members. It counts a lot when we look back and recall the help we have received along the way.

Commit to fathering even from the ashes. Choose to forgive the wrongs. Choose to be thankful for your fathering progress and the help of others. Choose to look toward the future of your fathering with hope. Whether you were the victim or perpetrator, choose life, choose love, choose fathering.

Chapter Twelve: Fathering the Broken

I wonder what Pastor Chris Komagum saw in me when I walked into his office in 1994 asking to be discipled. He was the associate pastor at Kampala Pentecostal Church (present-day Watoto Church) and was a very busy man. He had to preach through three or so Sunday services and oversee lots of administrative issues alongside having to meet scores of people who needed his wisdom and counsel.

I was quite a package. I was a very opinionated teenager with a low self-esteem who often embellished the truth. If I told a story of a movie and someone followed up to watch it, they would be left wondering why many of the parts I had told were not in the movie. I always seemed to have the extended version of the movie. Well, not really. That's called lying. So that was the package of a lad that I was.

I was opinionated because I did not want my little exposure to life to be questioned. So I asserted myself emphatically. At this point, I also still had the fight on my hands to prove to my father and the whole world that I was not stupid. So I embellished the truth in order to fit in.

From when I was ten, I had grown up in a house that did not have a TV. So, I colored my imagination with long tales much to my embarrassment, although I did not know at the time that the joke was on me.

I once told a friend and her sisters about using a deodorant for shoes. I obviously was found out to my shame. In the early nineties, there was no such thing. I hope someone can come up with such a product to vindicate my colorful imagination.

I had a low self esteem because I came from a broken family and was experiencing poverty in the midst of the lavishness that my school friends enjoyed. I could not explain why I always had to walk home or find a commuter taxi while my friends were either picked up in plush cars or they drove to the meetings we had when they grew older.

This was the young man that was asking Chris Komagum to father him. I was a mess even though I did my best to dress smart and look nice. I always dressed well (courtesy of thrift shop type clothes from the famous Owino market). I kept up with the latest hair cuts in town and was involved in an all-boy music group called Heaven Bound. I tried to look as cool as possible with all my insecurities and flaws neatly tucked away on the inside.

Chris Komagum and his wife Heather are really special people. They are the most vulnerable leaders I have met. In the season that he fathered me, there is barely a thing that I did not know about Pastor Chris Komagum. He gathered a number of young people whom he decided to father and mentor as a group. Dan Ruhweza, Clare Katwesigye (Now Mrs Ruhweza), Jack Musaali, Miriam Ekirapa (Now Mrs Musaali), Ronald Aziirwe, Alex Jakana, myself and a few others always met with Pastor Chris to pray with him at 6am every Tuesday morning during our school holidays.

We prayed for a while and shared what was going on in our lives then prayed in closing before we left. It was in this forum that many of us got to update him and each other on what was going on at home and in our lives. He had many hopes in us. He often spoke highly of us and encouraged us in the hearing of many.

He also did what many church leaders of his day and many now still find difficult to do. He opened up about his struggles, his weaknesses and disappointments. We prayed through a court case he had in his village over a long period of time till we saw victory. He shared his slip ups. He honestly talked to God about them in all our hearing. He prayed to God for his family, his work, his house, everything. He laid it all bare before us. There are not many leaders I respect as much as I respect this man.

He managed to get to the bottom of our messes by sharing his own. He inspired us to achieve much greater through his humility. It is from his mouth that I heard how he started participating in church leadership. At some point, he helped in cleaning the church toilets among other roles that he played. He showed himself faithful and Pastor Gary Skinner called him up to lead alongside him. He was and is still humble enough to acknowledge Pastor Gary Skinner as his mentor.

His name, Komagum, means the blessed one. Oh, what a blessing this man was to us. He fathered with humility and strength. His limp while he walked was a constant testimony of a man that had been battered by the storms of life but come to shore nonetheless because of his firm belief in God's hand, always turning things out for the good of those who love Him and are the called according to His purposes.

So when Chris Komagum implored us to be FAT, we had no excuses. FAT was a popular acronym that he used, which stood for being Faithful,

Available and Teachable. That was one of the lessons he drummed into us. He embodied being FAT in all ways. He spoke the truth always, kept his word, was there for all of us and was an avid, lifelong learner.

He gently and patiently got us to write down our life statements. In October 1996, He fathered me into writing down two very powerful statements that have defined my life: my life statement and the qualities I desired in my future spouse.

I wrote that I wanted to be a Good Family man (Father and Husband), a Good Pastor, a Good Businessman and a Good Friend. Unknown to me, for the last twenty years, this statement has been my lighthouse. It is what I have used to navigate my way through the storms of life. Every time I have made it to the shore, it has been because of this one statement.

Pastor Chris fathered me well enough to draw that out of me. He asked us to write down who we wanted to be and many years on, that's exactly what I am.

I am a pastor, involved in various businesses (Private and Government). I am a loyal friend to those I deem friends and have a lovely family life with my wife and children. This man fathered a very broken young boy and somehow got gold out of a mess of an ore. Many of my friends were not any better than me. They also had cheating or absentee fathers, wounded mothers, no focus, no guidance; the list goes on and on.

I recently reviewed the list of qualities that I desired in a spouse back then. To my exhilaration, my wife Lynnet scores big on all of them. Pastor Chris helped me find my wife and for that I am eternally grateful. These qualities are what mattered the most as I webbed through the treacherous waters of a youth trying to find a wife.

Broken people are highly sensitive and irrational. They will throw out the baby with the bath water when push comes to shove. That's what happened to me concerning this father of mine. It also happened to a young man I tried to father for twelve years.

In my case, I was hyper sensitive to being rejected. It brought out all my insecurities and I always responded by trying to be the one who ended a relationship. That is what helped me to cope with rejection or perceived rejection.

So at some point, I foolishly felt rejected by Pastor Chris and ended up straining a valuable father-son relationship.

Being a pastor now, I totally understand why pastors jealously guard their

Sunday afternoons. After a long grueling day of pouring out every bit of you into people's lives, you need to rest. The Sunday afternoon nap is any pastor's best kept trade secret. It is the best way to manage not being totally useless to yourself, your family and anyone else on Monday morning.

On behalf of all pastors and others who have to serve many people in the community, here is a plea: kindly respect their rest times. It is for both their good and yours.

My adventurous, spontaneous self took over me one Sunday afternoon. I took a taxi to Gaba (one of the suburbs of Kampala) to visit Pastor Chris unannounced. His guard asked to check whether Pastor Chris could see me and returned with a message that I should return some other time.

That really hurt me.

I am not sure he even knew a thing about this. His guard could even have been lying. So I sulked and walked away, feeling rejected, not realizing that I was at fault for not setting up an appointment. I therefore distanced myself because I needed to be in control of the overall call on whether the father-son relationship was over or not.

He continued to reach out to me and was one of the generous givers at my wedding in 2004. He is a father whose fathering I missed out on in my later years because I took offense. Looking back, I realize that all this was because I was a broken and messed up young man.

I would like to encourage any men who have attempted to father broken young people with little visible success. Yours is not a failed project. You have placed in them a lot more than you may be able to tell. There is a reason why God says that He is the rewarder of those who diligently seek Him. Mere men cannot really put into consideration all the sacrifices that you make for your broken children. No one knows your pain and no one can really pay you back but God.

For God is not unjust to forget your work and labor of love which you have shown toward His name, in that you have ministered to the saints, and do minister. (Hebrews 6:10)

Pastor Chris Komagum has a sure reward for his labor in my life. I have not honored him as much as I should have. I should have looked him up more. Even when I tried to have him to be one of the honored guests at my birthday when I made 33, his schedules could not allow it but God knows that his labor is not in vain.

I have fathered better because of him. I have been more vulnerable because of him. I have reached out more to the broken because of him. His reward is sure. Of that I have no doubt.

If you are fathering a difficult step child, an intolerable relative, a total stranger or a difficult young person to whom you are somehow drawn, do not give up on your effort.

Sometimes though, you need to realize that you have run your course. Sometimes it is pointless trying to pursue the person if they have decided to escape your love every single time you try. You need to rest in the knowledge that you have done your best. I sure hope to God that you make that call when you have tried your best.

I tried to father a young man for twelve years and at the end of that time, I felt like a complete failure. Even when I opened up every inch of me including my family and home, the relationship never got the depth I hoped for. It was mostly transactional. It was usually in times when he needed help that the fathering card was played. I felt so used and abused. I felt like an ATM machine.

I once had an animated conversation with him on phone concerning this very matter.

He responded in a typical broken person's style. He came home and took all his pictures and refused to talk to me for a while. We have tried to mend the relationship over time and it is nowhere near where it should be. History will judge as to whether I handled this one right.

I am not going to try to paint a picture of bliss when it comes to fathering the broken. Some of the people who adopt children get shocked when the children treat them as less than family after they grow older and are more independent. I have seen the pain in the eyes of some of these parents. This however cannot relegate us to the sidelines and stop us from fathering the broken.

God desires that all children are fathered. Whether they honor their fathers is up to them. We just have to do our part. It is for this reason that God says children should honor their parents.

Honor your father and your mother, that your days may be long upon the land which the Lord your God is giving you. (Exodus 20:12)

Moses, one of the most celebrated persons in the Bible, was born in a broken system to a broken set of parents. He grew up a broken person. A new ruler (Pharaoh) had decided to make Israelites slaves and ordered to have all their male babies killed for fear of how powerful the Israelites had become.

Born to slaves with a death warrant on his head, Moses survived by a whisker, only because an important person had compassion on his pitiful baby cry.

He was claimed by the Pharaoh's daughter at three months, given back to his mother to nurse him and then given to Pharaoh's daughter when he was older. It is not clear exactly how old he was when he was fully handed over to Pharaoh's daughter. The estimate by many Bible scholars is two to three years.

It must be noted that he probably was never told that these were his parents because if he was presented to Pharaoh's daughter and he claimed anyone else was his mother, his parents could have lost their lives.

Moses' father had to father that little boy, for that limited time, without disclosing his identity to him. It was stealth fathering and far from adequate.

We only get to know the effect of these few years with his father decades later, when Moses was forty years old. He was able to figure out that though he was raised Egyptian, in the line of power, probably a potential heir to the throne of Pharaoh, the Israelites were his brethren.

Stephen the first man martyred for his faith in Jesus Christ, in his address before his death, summarized Moses' life this way:

"Moses was learned in all the wisdom of the Egyptians, and was mighty in words and deeds.

"Now when he was forty years old, it came into his heart to visit his brethren, the children of Israel. And seeing one of them suffer wrong, he defended and avenged him who was oppressed, and struck down the Egyptian. For he supposed that his brethren would have understood that God would deliver them by his hand, but they did not understand.

"And the next day he appeared to two of them as they were fighting, and tried to reconcile them, saying, 'Men, you are brethren; why do you wrong one another?' But he who did his neighbor wrong pushed him away, saying, 'Who made you a ruler and a judge over us? Do you want to kill me as you did the Egyptian yesterday?' Then, at this saying, Moses fled and became a dweller in the land of Midian, where he had two sons.

"And when forty years had passed, an Angel of the Lord appeared to him in a flame of fire in a bush, in the wilderness of Mount Sinai. When Moses saw it, he marveled at the sight; and as he drew near to observe, the voice of the Lord came to him, saying, 'I am the God of your fathers—the God of Abraham, the God of Isaac, and the God of Jacob.' And Moses trembled and

dared not look. 'Then the Lord said to him, 'Take your sandals off your feet, for the place where you stand is holy ground. I have surely seen the oppression of My people who are in Egypt; I have heard their groaning and have come down to deliver them. And now come, I will send you to Egypt,'

"This Moses whom they rejected, saying, 'Who made you a ruler and a judge?' is the one God sent to be a ruler and a deliverer by the hand of the Angel who appeared to him in the bush. He brought them out, after he had shown wonders and signs in the land of Egypt, and in the Red Sea, and in the wilderness forty years. (Acts 7:22-36)

For the first forty years of his life, Moses was trained in all the wisdom of the Egyptians and was mighty in word and deed. According to Albert Barnes14, there may be substantial grounds for the tradition in Josephus that Moses was engaged in a military campaign against the Ethiopians, thus showing himself, as Stephen says "mighty in word and deed". So Moses was most probably a general in the army of Egypt.

His brokenness of identity would soon kick in and cause him to involuntarily murder an Egyptian official on government duty, the typical knee jerk reaction of a broken person.

Moses somehow knew that the Israelites were his brethren. The Bible does not tell us how he knew. Numerous Moses movies have given us countless angles. Could it have been the birth blanket, a nosy sister Miriam who broke into the palace one day and broke the news, or could it have been his very name, Moses, which means 'Drawn out of water'?

Could Moses have kept a memory of his very early years with his real family?

Is it possible that he recalled life with another family that was not Egyptian? Is it possible that he recalled his mother, his father, his sister Miriam and his brother Aaron? We can only speculate. What we know is he knew that he had Hebrew blood and was not willing to see an Egyptian mistreat his brethren anymore.

There is something about broken people that is straightforwardly redemptive. Broken people are usually unwilling to see the same brokenness and injustice that they experienced repeated. Broken people are uncompromising about the very same reason that they are broken.

It is no wonder that Moses ended up delivering the very same people from whom he was taken.

According to the account in Exodus, Moses killed the Egyptian official and hid him in the sand, hoping no one had seen him. When an Israelite exposed his action the next day and the Pharaoh also started actively looking for him to kill him, he fled to Midian. Moses' next forty years were spent with a Midian priest called Reuel Jethro, who became his father-in-law.

Having not really been fathered at forty, Moses needed to be fathered for forty years before he could go about the business of fathering the nation of Israel for another forty years.

His life is therefore divided into three segments. The first third of fatherlessness and belonging to a people that were not his own (the Egyptians). The second third was one of identifying with his people and being fathered by Jethro. The last third was about him fathering his own people, the nation of Israel. Each of those thirds was forty years. It seems to me that Moses could not father a nation before he himself had been fathered.

We cannot run short cuts around the need for the process of fathering. This is why we need Jethros. This is why we need men who are willing to father their own children and father other children too, most of who are broken. It is not possible to find a child who is not your own to father, who is not broken in some way. It is hard work to father this lot but be assured that your reward in fathering the broken is huge.

Broken people fail big but when they get it, they get it big. The list of broken men that got it big in the Bible is long: Abraham, Jacob, Judah, Joseph, Moses, Gideon, Samson, David, etc.

I can assure you that out of the hundreds of broken children you father, you will certainly get gems that make all your efforts worth it. That is the experience of men like Uncle Ben, John Bunjo, Chris Komagum, Gary Skinner and others who have been courageous enough to father the broken.

It is Jethro that took Moses in as a total stranger, loved him as his own and gave him a sense of real family.

Jethro fathered a runaway fugitive and a broken man. A man who had denied his royal privileges, identified with his slave roots, murdered an officer of Pharaoh, been rejected by his own and was hunted by the known world's super power army. If you were caught harboring this fugitive, the long arm of the law would take you along with him. Many would turn down the opportunity to father that kind of man, a forty year old at that. But not Jethro.

Moses honored Jethro as one would his own father. Even after God had instructed Moses at the famous burning bush, to go to Egypt, he first sought

Jethro's permission go.

So Moses went and returned to Jethro his father-in-law, and said to him, "Please let me go and return to my brethren who are in Egypt, and see whether they are still alive."

And Jethro said to Moses, "Go in peace." (Exodus 4:18)

Moses was uncircumcised. His parents had no time for ceremonies, especially when every Egyptian sought to kill every Hebrew baby boy. They hatched a plan to have him float on the Nile in order to preserve his life. If he had been found circumcised by an Egyptian, he would have been killed.

So God had just commissioned Moses to go to Egypt but then soon after found need to kill him. Here is how his quick-thinking wife Zipporah saved his life.

Now the Lord said to Moses in Midian, "Go, return to Egypt; for all the men who sought your life are dead." Then Moses took his wife and his sons and set them on a donkey, and he returned to the land of Egypt. And Moses took the rod of God in his hand.

And the Lord said to Moses, "When you go back to Egypt, see that you do all those wonders before Pharaoh which I have put in your hand. But I will harden his heart, so that he will not let the people go. Then you shall say to Pharaoh, 'Thus says the Lord: "Israel is My son, My firstborn. So I say to you, let My son go that he may serve Me. But if you refuse to let him go, indeed I will kill your son, your firstborn."'"

And it came to pass on the way, at the encampment, that the Lord met him and sought to kill him. Then Zipporah took a sharp stone and cut off the foreskin of her son and cast it at Moses' feet, and said, "Surely you are a husband of blood to me!" So He let him go. Then she said, "You are a husband of blood!"—because of the circumcision.

(Exodus 4:19-26)

It is Jethro who gave Moses a wife and subsequently a family. If you are Moses, you want to thank God for Zipporah and Jethro's fathering over her, especially when God seeks to kill you. Zipporah was most probably trained by her father concerning God's command to Abraham. (See Genesis 17:13-14).

According to Steve Rodeheaver[15], It appears that God was about to kill Moses because Moses was not circumcised. The episode takes place while Moses, his wife Zipporah, and their sons are lodging for the night. As Moses comes under attack by God, Zipporah takes a flint knife and circumcises their son.

Scripture says that she then takes their son's foreskin and touches Moses' feet with it. "Feet" is a Hebrew euphemism for "private parts." Every Hebrew reading or hearing the story would know that Zipporah did not touch Moses' "feet" with the foreskin, but his private parts. In this way she performed a vicarious circumcision, identifying Moses with the circumcision of their son. Upon this act the Lord "let him alone" and let Moses live.

So at this point, one of Moses' son's is circumcised and no good for the journey. Any man knows only too well how sensitive these matters can be. I believe this is why Moses sent his wife and two sons back to Jethro. The Bible does not mention Zipporah and Moses' children again in the story until they are brought back to Moses by Jethro after the Israelites had been delivered from the powerful grip of their Egyptian masters.

And Jethro, the priest of Midian, Moses' father-in-law, heard of all that God had done for Moses and for Israel His people—that the Lord had brought Israel out of Egypt. Then Jethro, Moses' father-in-law, took Zipporah, Moses' wife, after he had sent her back, with her two sons, of whom the name of one was Gershom (for he said, "I have been a stranger in a foreign land") and the name of the other was Eliezer (for he said, "The God of my father was my help, and delivered me from the sword of Pharaoh") (Exodus 18:1-4)

This is Moses' first mention of his biological father. Moses named his second son Eliezer, after the God of his father (the Levite) who by this point in the story is still unnamed. He acknowledges that it was his father's God who saved him from Pharaoh's sword.

Nonetheless, it is clear that it is Jethro who fathered Moses into his destiny to a point of supporting his family in the times when Moses had to risk his life and fight Egypt, the world's super power of the time. Jethro supported him to contend with Egypt only based on Moses' faith in a God who described Himself as 'I am'.

What Jethro did for Moses is akin to what grandfathers have to do in many parts of the world, looking after their grandchildren in order to allow their sons or daughters to figure things out in life; trying to stabilize their business startups, getting a job, or the like. This is what my maternal grandfather did for my mother. In times of turmoil in her marriage and times of being absolutely broke, he took us under his wing until things got better.

The Bible does not tell us how long it took for Moses to wrestle all the people of Israel out of the grip of the mighty Pharaoh and his army. We know that from when Moses departed Midian, there were ten plagues unleashed upon Egypt, including the killing of all the firstborns of Egypt. There was the crossing of the Red Sea, making the bitter waters at Marah sweet, provision of bread from heaven (Manna) and the striking of the rock of Horeb for water to nourish the over two million ex-slaves in the desert alongside a mighty victory in Israel's first battle against the Amalekites. That does not sound like stuff that takes a few weeks to accomplish.

Jethro had fathered a broken Moses. He had even borne the brunt of dealing with his sons and having to double the grandfather and the father role in order to support Moses' dream, vision and passion to deliver the Israelites. Jethro believed in Moses. The Bible does not mention at any single time that Jethro discouraged Moses on his mission to deliver Israel. He supported him and fathered him through it all.

The Bible does not say how old Moses' sons were at the time he received them back from Jethro. We know that when he first went to Midian, Moses stayed with Jethro who gave him one of his seven daughters, Zipporah, to marry. We know that they had had two sons by the time Moses left for Egypt to redeem the Israelites. We know that was about forty years after he married Zipporah. I imagine that his sons had probably been in their teen age or early twenties by the time Zipporah circumcised one of them and Moses had to send them back to Jethro in order to focus on the battle with Egypt.

And Jethro, Moses' father-in-law, came with his sons and his wife to Moses in the wilderness, where he was encamped at the mountain of God. Now he had said to Moses, "I, your father-in-law Jethro, am coming to you with your wife and her two sons with her."

So Moses went out to meet his father-in-law, bowed down, and kissed him. And they asked each other about their well-being, and they went into the tent. And Moses told his father-in-law all that the Lord had done to Pharaoh and to the Egyptians for Israel's sake, all the hardship that had come upon them on the way, and how the Lord had delivered them. (Exodus 18:5-8)

In what is the highest honor that Moses is known to have paid to any human being, he bowed down before Jethro when he met him again and kissed him.

Moses, in a typical report of a son to a father, reported all that they had gone through; the hardships and how God had delivered them from them all. That can only be a father-son conversation. If Jethro was nothing like a father, Moses would have postured and not spoken of the hardships. It is your father that you tell about your lows.

Jethro must have showed Moses how to be a priest and stand before God on behalf of a people. I believe that Jethro literally coached Moses in his destiny; for Moses always stood before God on behalf of the people of Israel in his last forty years. Jethro was a priest in Midian who could perform priestly duties before the God of Israel. Here is an account of Jethro's priesthood in action before all the elders of Israel.

Then Jethro rejoiced for all the good which the Lord had done for Israel, whom He had delivered out of the hand of the Egyptians. And Jethro said, "Blessed be the Lord, who has delivered you out of the hand of the Egyptians and out of the hand of Pharaoh, and who has delivered the people from under the hand of the Egyptians. Now I know that the Lord is greater than all the gods; for in the very thing in which they behaved proudly, He was above them."

Then Jethro, Moses' father-in-law, took a burnt offering and other sacrifices to offer to God. And Aaron came with all the elders of Israel to eat bread with Moses' father-in-law before God. (Exodus 18:9-12)

It is Jethro who gave Moses a brother from another mother in Hobab, his brother-in-law. Moses clearly loved Hobab and asked him to join them in the journey toward Canaan, promising that the same good that the Lord would do to the Israelites, they would do to him. Hobab was actually the desert guide of the whole nation of Israel as they sojourned through the desert. (See Numbers 10:29-36)

Hobab was a son of a priest (Jethro), most likely trained in priestly duties, concerning how to deal with God but more importantly, he knew the desert well. So he was comfortable walking at the front of the nation of Israel, guiding their footsteps, with the cloud of the LORD above him, guiding the nation's overall movement under Moses' leadership.

We see the mark of Jethro's fathering over Moses when he pulled him aside and admonished him like a father would a son. Moses listened to Jethro's admonition concerning delegating authority and obeyed. Jethro had fathered a broken Moses to the place he was and was literally throwing in a final lesson. (see Exodus 18:13-27)

Jethro most probably had many run-ins with Moses over the forty years that he fathered him.

It is not easy to father a man who is broken on the inside but has a lot to cover it up on the outside.

The first time Jethro met him, Moses must have spoken with Egyptian palatial sophistication, had the swag of a conquering general and spoken like one who had a post-doctoral qualification for he was well-trained in all the wisdom of the Egyptians.

It took modern-day scientists a while to figure out how to build the pyramids or how to embalm the dead and keep their bodies intact for thousands of years as the ancient Egyptians did. It is wisdom that almost sounds mythical. There is more that is discovered every year about the wisdom of ancient Egypt.

Jethro had to work through all that external charisma to get to the broken man that needed a real father.

So do not be intimidated by the externals. Some of the children you must father look too impressive to need your fathering. Others look more like a lost cause that makes you wonder why you should even try to father them. Whatever package they come in, father them.

When the scripture speaks about love, it says love never fails. Fathering is loving, period. If you choose to love and father the broken, you will not fail. Moses is living proof of a broken man that was fathered into a great man. In our day and age, there are many not so significant men that keep answering the great call of fathering. Out of their noble efforts come great leaders in all the nations of the world. Out of their efforts, they reap the Gold in Fathering.

Will you be one of these fathers? Will you father the Moses types for the next generation?

Chapter Thirteen: Fathering an Inheritance

Inheritance.

A word the Indian community in East Africa and beyond totally gets. You see them pass on to the next generation what they know and own. If you ever studied with an Indian in school, you will realize that they are students by day and business people by evening. It does not matter how old they are. That is fathering in one of its best and purest forms.

I have heard a story about the original Madhvani who came to Uganda with nothing but the clothes on his back and a few rupees in 1933. After passing on an inheritance between four generations, the Madhvanis are a household name in Uganda, very wealthy and powerful. They are influential and rich not just by Ugandan standards but also by British and Canadian standards too. That's rich. And that's because they understand inheritance. Inheritance is every bit part of the gold that our children ought to get from our fathering.

Here is one of the Bible's most captivating stories on fathering an inheritance.

In those days Hezekiah was sick and near death. And Isaiah the prophet, the son of Amoz, went to him and said to him, "Thus says the Lord: 'Set your house in order, for you shall die and not live.'"

Then Hezekiah turned his face toward the wall, and prayed to the Lord, and said, "Remember now, O Lord, I pray, how I have walked before You in truth and with a loyal heart, and have done what is good in Your sight." And Hezekiah wept bitterly.

And the word of the Lord came to Isaiah, saying, "Go and tell Hezekiah, 'Thus says the Lord, the God of David your father: "I have heard your prayer, I have seen your tears; surely I will add to your days fifteen years. I will deliver you and this city from the hand of the king of Assyria, and I will defend this city."' And this is the sign to you from the Lord, that the Lord will do this thing which He has spoken: "Behold, I will bring the shadow on the sundial, which has gone down with the sun on the sundial of Ahaz, ten degrees backward." So the sun returned ten degrees on the dial by which it had gone down.

Now Isaiah had said, "Let them take a lump of figs, and apply it as a poultice on the boil, and he shall recover."
(Isaiah 38: 1-8, 21)

It is important for us to note here that God is interested in every man leaving his house in order. God is not interested in the confusion that usually follows the demise of many men. The all too common stories of property grabbing by relatives and friends is not God's way. We are meant to leave a will that can be executed by the administrators of our estates.

Some men are scared of writing a will because they fear this would be pronouncing their own death. This is a fallacy. Having a will is one of the best gifts you can leave your surviving relatives.

My uncle, Isaac Matovu, was a man whose will was well known by everyone long before he passed away. His was a living will and there was no doubt in the mind of any of his relatives what was to become of his estate. Every child knew what their inheritance was.

Another man I know that had a living will was Sam Munywevu. In 1994 when he started Crane Crafts and Engravers Ltd, the leading engraving, signage and stamp making company in Uganda, he started it with his wife Anne. He involved his children in every aspect of the business during their school holidays and when his oldest son was at the University.

In August 2004 when he prematurely succumbed to a cardiac arrest and passed on, there was no doubt what was to happen to his wealth and business. His wife assumed leadership of the business and passed it on to the next generation. The Munywevu children, led by Simeon, have done so well running the business. A little over a decade since their father died, the company is much stronger and bigger than he left it. He passed on an inheritance of a business to children he had fathered to take it on and grow it. He must be extremely proud of them from where he is watching them.

Hezekiah had a boil that was going to kill him, but he desired longevity. He desired to see the goodness of God in the land of the living. He wept bitterly when Isaiah the prophet pronounced that his days were numbered. His pitch to God was "Remember now, O Lord, I pray, how I have walked before You in truth and with a loyal heart, and have done what is good in Your sight."

God answered his prayer in the affirmative but it is rather peculiar to see why this was a simple thing for God to do. God did this because of David! David was Hezekiah's forefather. In David's name, Hezekiah had an inheritance (see 2 Samuel 7:1- 17). You see, God had made a covenant with David that his

throne would last forever. The inheritance of a father's good name is not to be taken lightly.

The first time I met Sam Mutono at the World Bank offices in Kampala, I left his office with one thing on my mind: to tell everyone I met about him. I told my wife, my business partner, my friends and anyone who cared to listen, "I have met a man who reminds me of Jesus."

Sam is a humble man who makes close friends with people from all walks of life. He stops for everyone regardless of the caliber of person that he is. His meekness is disarming. Even when he knows lots more than anyone in the country about a particular technical issue, you will find him consulting people. He would even consult a novice like I was in the Water and Sanitation Sector about a decade ago. I sometimes wonder whether he really needs to or it is his way of empowering others. I have not seen anyone father careers and technical knowledge in a country as well as Sam Mutono has done in Uganda.

As a young, brilliant engineer, he went straight from his university to becoming the deputy head of Uganda's biggest Water and Sanitation project (RUWASA) in the late eighties. He would soon be promoted to head the project in the nineties. He has always been a leader, right from his school days at Ntare school and over the years, his leadership has culminated into leading Uganda's Sanitation sub sector.

On first sight, you would not imagine that this simple looking man is a deep well of wisdom and one of the best leaders Uganda has ever had. By my estimation, he has fathered more than 50% of all key leaders in the Water and Sanitation sector in the country. It is not uncommon to hear key thought leaders in the sector share stories about when they were working with Sam and how he coached and mentored them.

Having studied in the same school as Uganda's president and Rwanda's president, you would imagine that he would push his weight around, flaunting his credentials and connections as many lobbyists would do in our part of the world. Not Sam Mutono. He is different. That is why his name wields lots of respect in the Water and Sanitation sector in Uganda and in East Africa.

On October 3rd 2008, when our daughter Sinza was born, he was the only staff member from the World Bank who came to see us and wish us well. I know for a fact that he is a very busy man. He did not have to come. He was my boss. He owed me nothing but he still came. On 27th December 2010, when my father-in-law passed away in our house, Sam Mutono was there for the night vigil. He has always been there.

You may think me special and highly favored by this giant of a man. In some respect I think so but then again, you need to see him with everyone else. I believe that they too feel as special. That's who he is. He is consistent, reliable, loyal, humble, meek and an enduringly strong leader and father.

Having met me as a bright eyed young man from the private sector, he coached me into the development world. I came in knowing nothing about Sanitation and Hygiene but after nearly a decade, I am an expert in Hand Washing and, to a good extent, Sanitation and Sanitation marketing. I sat in his office with him and he studied me from a safe distance but was always close enough to father me. I am a better man because of this amazing father in our nation.

All his great exploits notwithstanding, it is the weight of Sam Mutono's name that surprises me. I have been stuck at work or in other scenarios and all he did was call or email the person concerned. In a few minutes doors that were impossible to open previously, flung open. If Sam Mutono is your father, you have an inheritance in his name. If Sam Mutono decides to cover you with his name, you have a great inheritance. Having been the National Hand Washing Coordinator in Uganda (2006-2014), I can tell you that this man's name is bankable.

Before God, Hezekiah had an even much greater inheritance in the name of David his father. It is that name that God invoked when he decided to heal Hezekiah and add fifteen years to his life.

At that time Merodach-Baladan the son of Baladan, king of Babylon, sent letters and a present to Hezekiah, for he heard that he had been sick and had recovered. And Hezekiah was pleased with them, and showed them the house of his treasures—the silver and gold, the spices and precious ointment, and all his armory—all that was found among his treasures. There was nothing in his house or in all his dominion that Hezekiah did not show them.

Then Isaiah the prophet went to King Hezekiah, and said to him, "What did these men say, and from where did they come to you?"

So Hezekiah said, "They came to me from a far country, from Babylon."

And he said, "What have they seen in your house?"

So Hezekiah answered, "They have seen all that is in my house; there is nothing among my treasures that I have not shown them."

Then Isaiah said to Hezekiah, "Hear the word of the Lord of hosts: 'Behold, the days are coming when all that is in your house, and what your fathers have accumulated until this day, shall be carried to Babylon; nothing shall be left,' says the Lord. 'And they shall take away some of your sons who will descend from you, whom you will beget; and they shall be eunuchs in the palace of the king of Babylon.'"

So Hezekiah said to Isaiah, "The word of the Lord which you have spoken is good!" For he said, "At least there will be peace and truth in my days." (Isaiah 39:1-8)

Hezekiah unfortunately went off the rails. He turned his testimony into a bragging parade to the Kingdom of Babylon and did the unthinkable. He bore all to them and showed them everything there was to know about Israel! He displayed the entire treasury and their entire armory! No one does that. Even with the pomp of military parades in many nations of the world today, no one really displays all their military force. No one opens up all their strategic and tactical advantages to potential enemies.

Hezekiah treated the hard-fought for secrets of his forefathers with disdain. In a bid to brag, he brought scorn upon the house of David. He treated his inheritance as worthless. Foreign kings and their dignitaries were never allowed into the sacred chambers of the palace. They never ever got to see all the wealth and military

ingenuity of generations before. That was an inheritance set apart only for the children of Israel, for the kings of Israel.

It's not wise to let it all out to everyone. Not all are friends. Not all wish you well and certainly not all need to know the inner workings of your business or vision.

Open it up only to people who will value it and keep you thankful to God for your progress, not those who will make you think that it's all because of you. That's because pride comes before a fall. You must stay grounded.

Be sure to keep some things exclusively for your heirs to know. Imagine what would happen if the Coca-Cola recipe went public 30 years ago. There would be no Coke now. I am not encouraging meanness. I am encouraging valuing what you have, God's role in your success and the importance of the inheritance from a father.

My maternal grandfather left an inheritance of lots of real estate for his children and his grand children. To this day, some of his children have his inheritance as part of their main source of income. What we leave for the generation after us matters. It is the stepping stone to thrust them deep into the future.

So after King Hezekiah's chest thumping parade, God said through Isaiah that all the gold his fathers had worked for and accumulated (for his inheritance and the inheritance of his descendants after him) would be taken away to Babylon. His descendants would also be made eunuchs (castrated and not able to sire children) and carried off to Babylon. His lineage and posterity was also at risk.

Hezekiah responded with the most absurd of responses in Isaiah 39:8: "At least there will be peace and truth in my days."

This is one of the most mindless statements I have read in the Bible. In one action, he was blowing away the inheritance, which generations before him had accumulated for him and those after him. In that one action, he was also putting the lives of his children, grand children and the entire nation in jeopardy. And what does he say? At least there will be peace and truth in my days!

When his life was in danger Hezekiah pleaded with God to save it but when generations after him were in danger, he thought it good considering he would not be affected. He never once tried to plead with God to change His mind about his descendants. He cared less about what inheritance he was to leave them. We can't be this kind of father. We need to leave an inheritance for our children and their children.

Proverbs 13:22a says that a good man leaves an inheritance to his children's children. No matter how old you are, you must start thinking about generations after you. You must start thinking about what inheritance you are leaving them. You must start thinking like a father.

Are you leaving a Godly heritage? Are you leaving circumstances better than you found them? Romans 8:16-17a says, *"The Spirit bears witness with our spirit that we are children of God, and if children, then heirs – heirs of God and joint heirs with Christ."*

Even God left us an inheritance that is everlasting and gains value every moment. An inheritance of Himself and everything that Jesus redeemed by His redemptive death and resurrection.

Inheritance matters. Think about it. Plan for it and execute it as a daily reality. In his book, _Called to Greatness: Embracing the Journey to Your Purpose and Destiny_, Moses Mukisa speaks about this area with depth and lots of wisdom. He calls it perpetuating greatness.

Inheritance matters. You are not living life for just yourself. You are living for your children and your children's children. Think Inheritance. Your inheritance can be a good name, a specialized skill, a well executed vision, a really cool product or a patent. Whatever it may be, I hope to God that your inheritance is translatable into financial terms whenever necessary, because money answers all things. The future generations need answers that only you and I can provide. Father them with a great inheritance. That will be Gold in your Fathering that they will be eternally grateful for.

Allow me say this especially to Christian men. God wants you rich. It is wrong to be thinking that poverty somehow endears you to God. If you are not rich you leave your children in jeopardy. They have to start off at the bottom of the pile. We must be wealthy and teach our children to harness that wealth and be richer than us. We must change the tide and hand down better stakes than many of our forefathers did. Insisting on poverty and a poverty mindset is no different from Hezekiah. There are three books that I would recommend for you to pick up and read right after this one. *Money Won't Make You Rich* by Sunday Adelajah, *Wealth Files* by Moses Mukisa and *Secrets of the Millionnaire Mind* by T. Harv Ekker.

There is so much money in the world; enough for all of us to have a lot of it. T. Harv Ekker compares it to rain. It is abundant and pours everywhere. If you choose to shelter yourself from it and not trap it, it will flow to someone else who will have more and more of it. Start or join a business and trap as much money as you can. Invest in something that multiplies your money. Do something.

We shall never fulfill the mandate of God's kingdom here on earth without possessing wealth. I personally had lots of unhelpful thinking concerning wealth. I am fighting these off with the tenacity of a tiger. I will be rich or die trying. There must be an inheritance left for my children and their children.

I have grown up with a 'just enough' thinking. The blueprint in my mind has been comfortable with having just enough to get by. Just enough fuel, just enough milk, just enough space, just enough!

I was raised by a single mother from when I was ten years old. She was a secretary and made an equivalent of 109 US dollars (Four hundred thousand Uganda shillings) per month. Clearly that was not enough for her four children. It was not enough for school fees, food, comfortable clothing, medication, etc. I regularly bought 'new' clothes from the old clothes passed down from Europe on the Owino market floor. At times I would skip mentioning that I was unwell in order to save the family resources from being spent on treatment and medication.

When you come from the land of not enough, just enough is more than fine. Life is so much better. You are on cloud nine. The problem with this state of mind, however, is that, it is not what God's heart is for you and me. God has pleasure in the prosperity of His people. (See Psalm 35:27)

Prosperity does not read like just enough from where I stand. Prosperity brings to mind abundance.

Being in the church circles that I grew up in did not help my "just enough" mentality. Here is one of the most memorized and preached about scriptures back then:

Now godliness with contentment is great gain. For we brought nothing into this world, and it is certain we can carry nothing out. And having food and clothing, with these we shall be content. But those who desire to be rich fall into temptation and a snare, and into many foolish and harmful lusts which drown men in destruction and perdition. For the love of money is a root of all kinds of evil, for which some have strayed from the faith in their greediness, and pierced themselves through with many sorrows. (1 Timothy 6:6-10, emphasis mine)

We were told in very subtle ways that being rich is wrong. In fact desiring to be rich is equal to wanting out of heaven or the things of God. We were told that being rich is loving money which is the source of all evil. We were told that wanting to be rich is greediness which is a sin. How wrong!

The scripture spoke of contentment in contrast with greed. It's better to be contented with what God has given you as compared to being greedy, wanting to grab everything in your sight. This is the kind of greed that gets one swindling resources from their public office just because they can.

This scripture does not say it is okay to be greedy. It also does not say it is okay to be poor or to have just enough. It does not!

In fact there is a scripture that speaks quite well of money.

A feast is made for laughter, And wine makes merry; But money answers everything. (Ecclesiastes 10:19)

We cannot go about life successfully without money. We need it to get by concerning almost everything. This scripture does not say just enough. It puts no limit to the amount of money.

There was yet another scripture for the just enough crowd, which I have belonged to for so long.

And my God shall supply all your need according to His riches in glory by Christ Jesus. (Philippians 4:19, emphasis mine)

The wrong mentality here is that God only supplies

my needs.

This is very wrong! The supply is according to his riches in glory! That spells O.V.E.R.F.L.O.W. I can guarantee you that God is not broke, making do with only one robe. The testimony of those that have seen God does not paint a broke picture. He wraps Himself in light! Can you picture that? No man has been that rich yet! His streets are made of gold. The foundation of the city of heaven that He is working on has many precious stones! He travels in a chariot that has wheels, which move in every direction. He is so amazing to look upon that the 24 elders continuously fall to their knees, lay down their golden crowns and cry, "Holy, Holy, Holy are you Lord!"

That's not broke. That's not just enough. That's more than enough. That's abundance!

It is a culture in the Kingdom of God to give. We are royalty as children of God. Generosity is our style. I assume that this is an obvious truth and that you regularly tithe, give, first fruit, or whichever format you use for generosity.

Here is another scripture that completely disqualifies the "just enough" mentality:

But this I say: He who sows sparingly will also reap sparingly, and he who sows bountifully will also reap bountifully. So let each one give as he purposes in his heart, not grudgingly or of necessity; for God loves a cheerful giver. And God is able to make all grace abound toward you, that you, always having all sufficiency in all things, may have an abundance for every good work. (2 Corinthians 9:6-8, emphasis mine)

God is able to give you all manner of special ability or gifting in business and innovation that enables you to have all sufficiency in all things (that's the just enough level) and an abundance for every good work (that's the prosperity level).

We were never meant to just survive, having just enough. That is ground zero. Ours is meant to be abundance.

Let the peoples praise You, O God; Let all the peoples praise You. Then the earth shall yield her increase; God, our own God, shall bless us. God

shall bless us, And all the ends of the earth shall fear Him.
(Psalm 67:5-7, emphasis mine)

Imagine that kind of blessing. It is the kind of blessing that the owners of the Emirates enjoy right now. It is the kind that Bill Gates and other billionaires enjoy. This is the kind of blessing that causes many to fear. That does not feel like just enough. That feels like more than enough.

Bring all the tithes into the storehouse, That there may be food in My house, And try Me now in this," Says the Lord of hosts, "If I will not open for you the windows of heaven And pour out for you such blessing That there will not be room enough to receive it. (Malachi 3:10)

The kind of blessing God has available for you and me is that kind where the windows of heaven open and pour on you. So much that you have no room to keep it. I hope you realize that tithes and offerings come from some source of income: a business, farm or investment. You can't just pray the blessings into being. You must have a money making vehicle to get there.

I have kissed my "just enough" mentality goodbye. In fact, I am not being civil about it. I have divorced myself from it and will battle any remnants of it that keep me locked up in just enough.

I need to have enough space in my mind to take in the abundance. I must think big. I must enlarge my tent. I must increase my capacity to receive.

I honestly hope that is your story too. I hope that is exactly what you have determined because you must father your children with an inheritance. I sure hope to God that it won't be just two chickens and a goat.

Chapter Fourteen: Fathering Nations and Generations

On June 24th 2015, we drove into Redding, California, for our very first time. My friend, Alex Mutagubya, his five year old daughter Aaliyah and I had been on the road for over six hours. It had been a long drive from Bend, Oregon but I quickly forgot the strain it had had on us.

I excitedly jumped out of the car and was greeted by the hot California sun, right outside the Bethel Media offices. We took pictures and I am certain that I beamed the most. This was a dream come true.

I had hoped and dreamt about visiting Bethel Church for years. Moses Mukisa, our senior pastor at Worship Harvest Ministries, had visited Bethel four years before and returned with raving reports about them. He carried some of their books which I quickly devoured. Lynnet had also attended their School of Prophets conference the year before. I had been happy for her and could not wait for my turn. Lo and behold, I was in Redding!

I was super excited about Bethel and anyone associated with them. Through the friendship that Alex had with Pastor Keith Patrick and the wonderful congregation at The Journey Church in Bend, we had met an amazing couple, Johnny and Audrey. They had been our hosts while in Bend and had connected us through their friend to an amazing lady called Pam Spinosi.

Pam works with Bethel Church and we had just parked right in front of her office.

It was not long before Pam came to save us from the scorching sun, leading us into the Bethel media offices. The cool interior was welcoming.

She got us registered for the Kingdom Culture conference and checked us in at her house. We soon discovered that although she had just met us, she was leaving us her house with her precious cats for the entire time we would be in Redding! She stayed at a friend's house that whole time. She brought really important people to dine with us during our stay and literally opened her fridge to two able-bodied young men and a five-year-old girl. This was dumbfounding love and honor extended to a pair of young pastors visiting from Africa.

The evening session of the conference would be the beginning of the unraveling of Bethel Church's best kept secret. Bethel Church is known for miracles, signs and wonders; a revival culture as some would call it. If you have not been there, I would like to add my voice to many that these things are true. I did experience them. I saw legs growing, a flat foot made right among many others. They have a very strong prophetic culture and a culture of honor.

It is the culture of honor that is less trumpeted about Bethel and is, in my view, their strongest point. I got to see Bill Johnson and all the fathers of the Bethel House like Kris Vallotton, Danny Silk and Paul Manwaring in action. The rest of the key leaders like Kevin Dedmond, Chris Gore, Chris Overstreet, Eric & Candice Johnson and Jason Vallotton were no different. They all honored each other. No one was taken for granted at Bethel. The security personnel carried themselves with a regal and rare confidence. The numerous members of the congregation that prayed and ministered to the thousands of conference guests were no different.

Bill Johnson said that 95% of the miracles, signs and wonders were performed by the members of the congregation that stepped up to minister to others. It was not the leaders that did most of this amazing stuff we hear about. I saw a guy at the reception of the healing rooms pray over two legs that grew while he was going about the business of making us feel welcome.

Sandra Kane, a lady who ministered to me in prayer when I visited the Bethel Healing Rooms, introduced herself this way: "Hello, my name is Sandra. I am one of the mothers in this house."

It dawned on me then, as I had suspected from the time the first session of the conference had ended, that Bethel Church is one huge family with fathers and mothers through their ranks.

If one was in any doubt about this, you just need to watch and listen to Bill Johnson. He is the lead father of the house. He carries himself like a father, speaks like a father, encourages like a father and admonishes like a father. Bill Johnson literally oozes with the love of a father.

I could tell from his communication that he was running on a full tank of God the Father's love for him. During the conference and in Bethel Church's books or videos, it has been mentioned that Bill Johnson hangs onto every word of prophesy he receives. He revises those words over and over like his life depends on them. He is keen to have anyone who is experiencing the Father's love and power, different than him, to pray and prophesy over him. I would understand why. True prophecy should read like a love letter, like the communication of a general encouraging his troops at the frontline, like the assuring hug of a loving father.

From a man who has received the love of God the Father, we see a people that are loved by a father. From a man who is fathered, we hear and see great exploits from a people who have been fathered. The Gold in Fathering is Bethel Church's best kept secret. The culture of honor between fathers and their children (both biological and spiritual children) is Bethel Church's glue. That is the reason for their global influence.

So when I had an opportunity for Bill Johnson to pray over me, it is for fathering that I asked. It is that single most treasured responsibility and honor that I asked more of. If I could father like Bill Johnson fathers, I am certain I'd live a significant life.

His public ministry notwithstanding, Bill Johnson's fathering of his biological children is commendable. When you hear his son, Eric Johnson speak, you hear the wisdom and maturity of a man well-fathered. Yet here is a most interesting truth. Bill Johnson is a fifth generation church leader. His father, Earl Johnson, was a pastor before him and others were pastors before them.

I had the rare opportunity to visit the Bethel Church boardroom and it was clear that fathering sat at the heart of this amazing church movement. What struck me first was a small black chair that was among many plush, comfortable chocolate brown boardroom chairs. I asked the gentlemen we were with, "Whose chair is that little black one?" Without any hesitation they answered, almost in chorus, "Bill's."

I am from Africa and had seen and experienced my fill of hierarchical leadership. We have a chief mentality in most parts of our world. The leaders are lords over the people they are meant to serve. The young serve the old, often unquestionably. In Africa, sons serve fathers. Rarely is it the other way round.

I do not know why Bill's chair was smaller and shorter than anyone's chair in that boardroom. I do not want to speculate. I will just tell you what that made me feel. I felt that this is one of the humblest leaders there must be. It gives me the impression of a father who is willing to lay down his honor and privileges in order to honor and father others.

On the walls all around are pictures of revivalists of old. The A-list of God's generals that Roberts Liardon wrote about in his-all time classic books, God's Generals. They honor the revivalists that went before them. They accept the honor to father revival to the nations. They also honor each other from the greatest to the smallest.

I was most enthused when I heard the story of Bill Johnson and his son Eric. At first, I was a little bothered by the way Eric spoke. He was not as clear as most other speakers at the conference. For some reason, Eric and Candice Johnson are the Senior pastors of the Bethel local church and I wondered why.

I soon got to see their depth and passion for God. I was amazed when I heard that Eric was wearing hearing aids even as he led a local church with hundreds of miracles, signs and wonders performed every month.

Eric Johnson was born over 80% deaf in both his ears. Bill Johnson had prayed for his healing many times and was assured that his son would be healed. Eric grew up almost deaf but is leading this amazing local church.

Eric Johnson has prayed over countless deaf people who have received their healing instantly. Deaf ears being opened is the most frequent miracle that happens in Eric Johnson's ministry.

This screams to the highest heaven that this man has been fathered right. He has been fathered to believe in a God that loves and heals. He has been fathered to honor, love and serve others, regardless of his struggles or unfulfilled hopes. He has been fathered in the ways of royalty, never allowing to live below the standard of a child of God, a child of the King of Kings. That is the mark of Bill Johnson's fathering.

After Bill Johnson had prayed over me on the morning of Friday 26th June, 2015, I had no hopes in my mind that he remembered me after that, for he had many line up to pray over them and bless them.

Just after the afternoon breakout sessions, I was walking out and he was walking into the auditorium. I nodded to acknowledge him as he passed by and what followed was something I will never forget.

He stopped and put his right hand on my right shoulder (we were facing opposite directions) and he said, "Fathering in Uganda. Fathering in Uganda," while patting my shoulder.

From that point on, I knew that my passion for fathering was not a fickle matter. It was not just a childhood dream or an over compensation for the fathering I missed. It was not merely born out of the many pitiful cries that I have heard from others about the absence or passiveness of their fathers. I knew that it was God's heart that there would be fathering in my nation and, by extension, in every single nation on the earth.

I can tell you with confidence that God is interested in us fathering our children and the many fatherless children God brings our way. His purpose is that we represent Him so well as fathers that our children will be drawn to Him, the Father of All. There is no greater treasure than this. Fathering people to a level where, when they think of us, they think of God, is the highest level of fathering there is to attain.

And He has made from one blood every nation of men to dwell on all the face of the earth, and has determined their preappointed times and the boundaries of their dwellings, so that they should seek the Lord, in the hope that they might grope for Him and find Him, though He is not far from each one of us; for in Him we live and move and have our being, as also some of your own poets have said, 'For we are also His offspring.' (Acts 17:26-28)

We have been given the highest honor to father generations after us. Every man that walks this planet has this single and highest honor placed on his shoulders. This is true whether you have sired children of your own or not.

In Africa, we have a common saying, "It takes a village to raise a child." This was and, in some respects, is still true to this very day. When our parents were little children, all the men on their village were considered fathers in some respect. If they found children doing something mischievous, they would discipline them on the spot and later report the incident to their fathers.

It was an unwise child that would attempt to report a roadside disciplining incident to their father for then they would receive double for their trouble. Their own fathers would typically reinforce what the 'roadside father' had deemed fit. In that respect, the entire village watched out for every child and made sure they were raised right. There was a fathering culture and a clear picture that the whole society had and upheld of a well-fathered child.

A lot has changed since the 1940s. We are more individualistic and would typically not look kindly upon a stranger correcting our child, at least not in the way it was done in the last century. Yet we still have many among us who desire to be fathered; many who desire the invitation and challenge of a father. There are many who lack the boundaries and guidance that the love and discipline of fathers provides. It is said that when children are little, having no boundaries set for them makes them feel unloved, yet one would think the opposite these days. This ought not to be so. If you have the honor of fathering many, don't take it lightly.

Here is a peculiar saying by the sons of Korah:

A man who is in honor, yet does not understand, Is like the beasts that perish. (Psalm 49:20)

Honor comes in many shapes and sizes: wealth, political power and many other forms that definitely include fathering. Here the psalmists said that a man who is in honor and yet does not understand is no different from a cow or a goat. For cows and goats are not wise enough to think about their posterity. They do not secure their next generations by fathering them in the way they should go. Cows and goats need no coaching on how to be cows and goats. They have their basic instincts to take care of that but not so for human beings.

This is the reason we have words like legacy in our vocabulary. You can father generations if you choose to. You can father nations.

This is what I believe Uncle Ben has done in Uganda. Recently, Charity Kwatampora, a friend of mine and one of the leaders at church, shared this in an email group that I am part of:

"I have been thinking a lot lately about my relationship with Uncle Ben. I met him as a 7 year old girl. Our two families moved onto the Hill (Makerere University) at the same time, which fact God used to connect us. He was our person of peace as a whole family. His love for me has always been evident and constant. I doubt all those years ago, he was thinking of me ministering the gospel as the end result of our relationship. He loved me, answered my questions and acknowledged me regardless of the crowds of titled adults around him.

"A few weeks into 'my senior one first term, I wrote Uncle Ben about this new teaching that was worrisome—Evolution'— plus the major detail that I was in possession of a set of HB pencils with the number 666 (I thought I was unwittingly going to hell).

"He wrote me back. To this very day I recall it was 6 pages explaining Creation afresh and how God loved me and how Salvation works. He taught me about God and Faith whether it was in a letter or on the street or in his office or on the steps outside chapel.

"Surely I can do the same with hundreds of young people if I am willing."

This is the single and highest honor that all fathers carry; to multiply yourself and the greatness in you to many generations through your fathering. In your fathering the next generation and your nation is gold worth more than any other.

There is a lot to learn about fathering a nation from Joseph, the son of

Jacob.

The beginning of the book of Exodus gives us a picture on how far reaching Joseph's fathering was.

Now there arose a new king over Egypt, who did not know Joseph. And he said to his people, "Look, the people of the children of Israel are more and mightier than we; come, let us deal shrewdly with them, lest they multiply, and it happen, in the event of war, that they also join our enemies and fight against us, and so go up out of the land." Therefore they set taskmasters over them to afflict them with their burdens. And they built for Pharaoh supply cities, Pithom and Raamses. But the more they afflicted them, the more they multiplied and grew. And they were in dread of the children of Israel. So the Egyptians made the children of Israel serve with rigor. And they made their lives bitter with hard bondage—in mortar, in brick, and in all manner of service in the field. All their service in which they made them serve was with rigor.

Then the king of Egypt spoke to the Hebrew midwives, of whom the name of one was Shiphrah and the name of the other Puah; and he said, "When you do the duties of a midwife for the Hebrew women, and see them on the birthstools, if it is a son, then you shall kill him; but if it is a daughter, then she shall live." (Exodus 1:8-16)

According to Cambridge Bible for Schools and Colleges commentary, this king was Rameses II, the third ruler of the 19th dynasty (B.C . 1300 -1234). Bible scholars have calculated that the birth of Moses, when this king reigned, took place 279 years after Joseph's death.

This king was not acquainted with Joseph, did not remember his services, and had no thought or care for his people.

Ellicott's Commentary for English readers adds, "It seems to be implied that, for some considerable time after his death, the memory of the benefits conferred by Joseph upon Egypt had protected his kinsfolk."[16]

Joseph became the prime minister of Egypt at 30 years, his family moved to Egypt when he was 40 years old. Joseph died at 110 years[17]. For 349 years, the children of Israel prospered and grew in number in Egypt so much so that they became a two million strong nation that threatened the very existence of Egypt. All this was on the back of Joseph's fathering.

In a political manoeuvre with no precedent in Bible history, the new king decided to make the Israelites slaves and also kill their male children in an effort to stem their rapid influence as a people.

A noteworthy detail that recently caught my eye is how the Bible begins to narrate the history of Jacob. Jacob's history begins with the fathering dreams of his son, Joseph. That is really significant.

Now Jacob dwelt in the land where his father was a stranger, in the land of Canaan. This is the history of Jacob.

Joseph, being seventeen years old, was feeding the flock with his brothers. And the lad was with the sons of Bilhah and the sons of Zilpah, his father's wives; and Joseph brought a bad report of them to his father.

Now Israel loved Joseph more than all his children, because he was the son of his old age. Also he made him a tunic of many colors. But when his brothers saw that their father loved him more than all his brothers, they hated him and could not speak peaceably to him.

Now Joseph had a dream, and he told it to his brothers; and they hated him even more. So he said to them, "Please hear this dream which I have dreamed: There we were, binding sheaves in the field. Then behold, my sheaf arose and also stood upright; and indeed your sheaves stood all around and bowed down to my sheaf."

And his brothers said to him, "Shall you indeed reign over us? Or shall you indeed have dominion over us?" So they hated him even more for his dreams and for his words.

Then he dreamed still another dream and told it to his brothers, and said, "Look, I have dreamed another dream. And this time, the sun, the moon, and the eleven stars bowed down to me."

So he told it to his father and his brothers; and his father rebuked him and said to him, "What is this dream that you have dreamed? Shall your mother and I and your brothers indeed come to bow down to the earth before you?" And his brothers envied him, but his father kept the matter in mind. (Genesis 37:1-11)

Only for his mistake of telling on his brothers' misdoings do I fault Joseph. The rest of his story speaks of a father worth emulating in all ways.

He was a clear favorite, having been born to his father in his old age. When Joseph was seventeen, with this multi colored coat on, he reported dreams that depicted his brothers, father and mother bowing before him. In an already tense household, this was not a welcome gesture. Joseph had the nerve to pull this off twice!

These dreams spoke about Joseph's greatness. They spoke of the type of father he would be in his later years. The dreams told of Joseph being a father so great that his father and brothers, even though older, would bow down before him.

Joseph was labeled a dreamer. He survived being lynched by a mob of angry brothers and was sold into slavery.

We have all had Joseph dreaming moments and have many a time given up on them because they were too big, too scary in light of our abilities or they were too unbelievable for anyone to buy. Unfortunately for many men, the scorn of others has silenced our dreams to build multibillion dollar businesses that employ our entire nation, to write books that are read all over the world, to build defense and political mechanisms that literally bring wars to an end, to heal the sick and raise the dead.

Our world is brimming with bad news. The cynics rule the day. It seems like the weirder things get is the more the people around us celebrate. What is celebrity now leaves many genuine men hiding under their beds for fear of not being accepted and believed in. Critics run rife, never mind that they have not done any of the stuff they are criticizing. Entire professions have been built on criticizing instead of building up something.

If you have a Joseph type of dream and want to father something never seen or heard of before, take courage in the fact that the naysayers have never snuffed out a dream that burns so bright in the deep recesses of any man. Push back hard and believe in your God-given dream to father something bigger than you. Develop a thick skin and refuse to cower under the barrage of words that monger gloom and seek to discourage. Choose to father that big, audacious dream. History will prove you right and prove them wrong.

A lot of water went under Joseph's proverbial bridge. He moved from a freeman to a slave in Potiphar's house. He moved from a faithful servant to Potiphar to an alleged uncontrolled rapist. While in jail, Joseph was elevated to head up all the prisoners. His leadership qualities and his fathering were always bringing him to the top because the Lord was with him.

Joseph had a chance to get out of jail sooner when he correctly interpreted the dreams of two officers of the king, the chief butler and the chief baker. The chief butler who was restored could have remembered him but he didn't.

So Joseph was a forgotten slave in prison. Nothing could have been any lower than that. Imagine that you are owned by another man; a prison of its own kind. Reading up on slave trade and slavery in the Americas reveals the horrors of slave trade. The classic TV series 'Roots' does a good job bringing the evils of slavery to light. So in addition to slavery, Joseph was also in a physical prison and while at it, his only hope of exiting that situation was dashed by the King's chief butler who made a promise to say a kind word for him to the king but forgot all about him.

In our journey to father the dreams in our hearts, we are certainly faced with great challenges and disappointments. The challenges, though tough on us, never really weigh as heavy as the disappointments we get.

Have you ever realized that you cannot get to where you need to go without people, even the people who disappoint you?

Do not throw up your hands in the air and kiss your Joseph dream goodbye. For Joseph, his brothers had to sell him into slavery in order to catapult him into Egypt, the land of his dreams. Potiphar's wife had to accuse him falsely for him to make it into jail, for it was in the jail that he met the king's chief butler. When the king had disturbing dreams, the chief butler remembered Joseph, introduced him to the king and the rest was history.

Difficult as his journey to the actualization of his dreams might have been, there was no way better and more effective than what he experienced. For twenty years, Joseph was learning the ways of royalty. While serving Potiphar, the captain of the king's guard, Joseph learnt the mannerisms of royalty. He excelled so much in all he did that Potiphar put him in charge of his entire household. While in prison, he learnt more ways of royalty. He learnt a lot about the power and authority of Pharaoh that when he came out of there and was made the second man to Pharaoh, he used his position to maximum effect. I believe he knew exactly how to avoid wronging Pharaoh and ending up in jail again.

In the same respect, embrace your journey to your dreams. Embrace the difficulties and the disappointments from people. Don't keep a grudge. God is with you even as he was with Joseph. Do not despair.

It was God's being with Joseph through these dark days that helped him see things with perspective.

Commit to learning from every circumstance. Learn from people who are better than you. Learn from those who are worse off than you are. Learn from your mistakes and successes. Learn because true fathers pass on the lessons they have learnt in life. What differentiates a father from a peer is that he has a wealth of lessons and wisdom to glean from. The generations that follow ought not to suffer the same pain we have. They should be wealthier, wiser and grow older than us. That's progress.

Then Joseph could not restrain himself before all those who stood by him, and he cried out, "Make everyone go out from me!" So no one stood with him while Joseph made himself known to his brothers. And he wept aloud, and the Egyptians and the house of Pharaoh heard it.

Then Joseph said to his brothers, "I am Joseph; does my father still live?" But his brothers could not answer him, for they were dismayed in his presence. And Joseph said to his brothers, "Please come near to me." So they came near. Then he said: "I am Joseph your brother, whom you sold into Egypt. But now, do not therefore be grieved or angry with yourselves because you sold me here; for God sent me before you to preserve life. For these two years the famine has been in the land, and there are still five years in which there will be neither plowing nor harvesting. And God sent me before you to preserve a posterity for you in the earth, and to save your lives by a great deliverance.

So now it was not you who sent me here, but God; and He has made me a father to Pharaoh, and Lord of all his house, and a ruler throughout all the land of Egypt. (Genesis 45:1-8)

Joseph viewed the past twenty years of his ups and downs as God sending him to Egypt to make him a father to Pharaoh and Lord of his entire house and a ruler throughout all the land of Egypt.

All along, this is what the dreams were about. Joseph was to father the king of the world's super power at the time. He fathered the whole nation of Egypt and the budding nation of Israel. If God had pronounced these things to Joseph while he was much younger, it probably would have been pretty scary.

Jacob, his father, had rebuked him for his last dream but kept these things to his heart. Shocked as Jacob must have been to learn that his son was alive and a ruler of Egypt, he must have remembered the dreams.

Do not be afraid to talk about your dreams and visions. They will attract both lovers and haters and both these categories of people will work together to help you achieve your God-given dreams whether they desire to or not. Some will disappoint you and others will encourage you. Some will seek to pull you down and others will seek your wellbeing. Whichever way, in the end, it will all work out for your good.

In every one of us is a contribution that must be made on this planet before we breathe our last breath. In every one of us is an opportunity to father something that will last generations. In every one of us is an opportunity to father generations and nations.

Joseph did mighty exploits for Pharaoh on whose accord kindness was shown to the Israelites while in Egypt for over three centuries. Have you asked yourself how far reaching your fathering is?

Nothing beats Joseph's exploits and the meticulous execution of his fathering role over Pharaoh. Any Forbes 500 company would pay billions of US Dollars just to have Joseph accept the role of being their CEO. He was a genius and pointedly focused of fathering the Pharaoh to greatness.

Now there was no bread in all the land; for the famine was very severe, so that the land of Egypt and the land of Canaan languished because of the famine. And Joseph gathered up all the money that was found in the land of Egypt and in the land of Canaan, for the grain which they bought; and Joseph brought the money into Pharaoh's house.

So when the money failed in the land of Egypt and in the land of Canaan, all the Egyptians came to Joseph and said, "Give us bread, for why should we die in your presence? For the money has failed." Then Joseph said, "Give your livestock, and I will give you bread for your livestock, if the money is gone." So they brought their livestock to Joseph, and Joseph gave them bread in exchange for the horses, the flocks, the cattle of the herds, and for the donkeys. Thus he fed them with bread in exchange for all their livestock that year.

When that year had ended, they came to him the next year and said to him, "We will not hide from my Lord that our money is gone; my Lord also has our herds of livestock. There is nothing left in the sight of my Lord but our bodies and our lands. Why should we die before your eyes, both we and our land? Buy us and our land for bread, and we and our land will be servants of Pharaoh; give us seed, that we may live and not die, that the land may not be desolate."

Then Joseph bought all the land of Egypt for Pharaoh; for every man of the Egyptians sold his field, because the famine was severe upon them. So the land became Pharaoh's. And as for the people, he moved them into the cities, []from one end of the borders of Egypt to the other end. Only the land of the priests he did not buy; for the priests had rations allotted to them by Pharaoh, and they ate their rations which Pharaoh gave them; therefore they did not sell their lands.

Then Joseph said to the people, "Indeed I have bought you and your land this day for Pharaoh. Look, here is seed for you, and you shall sow the land. And it shall come to pass in the harvest that you shall give one-fifth to

Pharaoh. Four-fifths shall be your own, as seed for the field and for your food, for those of your households and as food for your little ones."

So they said, "You have saved our lives; let us find favor in the sight of my Lord, and we will be Pharaoh's servants." And Joseph made it a law over the land of Egypt to this day, that Pharaoh should have one-fifth, except for the land of the priests only, which did not become Pharaoh's.(Genesis 47: 13-26)

A father like Joseph was worth the highest honor especially if you were an Egyptian Pharaoh. There was no Pharaoh before who had ever owned the whole land of Egypt and its people. No Pharaoh had ever been made that rich and powerful. Joseph literally made the Pharaohs much more powerful than they had ever dreamt. He made them richer and wealthier too and this was done to gargantuan proportions. It was unthinkable and unimaginable what Joseph did for Pharaoh. That is what he meant when he said God had made him a father to Pharaoh and a ruler of all Egypt.

By the ideas and dreams in your heart, God has made you a father to some important people and to specific nations. God has placed gold in your hands by reason of the numerous sons and daughters that you are fathering, whether biological or not.

Joseph's Fathering was tied to the history of Jacob, his father. Jacob did nothing nearly as dumbfounding as his son Joseph, yet because he fathered Joseph, he was accorded the highest honor in Egypt. In a land where the Pharaoh was the source of all things good, the Pharaoh humbled himself to receive a blessing from Jacob. The Pharaoh so honored Joseph that he allowed Joseph's father to speak over him as his own son. (see Genesis 47:7-10)

We can all father generations and nations whether we are Josephs and Bill Johnsons or Jacobs and Earl Johnsons. We shall all eat of fathering benefits in our lifetimes but greater yet, when we are long gone, there is a possibility that we shall all be remembered for centuries like Joseph as men who took a hold of the Gold in Fathering.

Conclusion

I hope that this book has sparked a golden fire in your gut and given you the determination to father generations and nations. I hope that you have been encouraged not to give up on your fight for your place on the table of men that daily take hold of the Gold in Fathering. I hope that you have determined within yourself that you will not allow going down to your grave aiding the gloomy fatherlessness statistics that are mocking fathers globally.

Claude Nikondeha is one of the remarkable fathers we have in Africa. He is a man that has fathered African leaders through Amahoro Africa[18], fathered successful businesses out of impoverished people through Kazoza Finance[19] and changed the story of a much neglected people group through Communities of Hope[20].

When Claude visited the Batwa people in Burundi, he could not shake off their hunger and untold suffering, being an ostracized minority group that lived in abject poverty. No one really cared what happened to the Batwa. It was acceptable for the rest of Burundi to move forward while the Batwa people had no food, no economic means and a poor education for their children.

On his first visit to the Batwa, Claude literally had to crawl through the entrances of the Batwa's houses and wondered how an entire family could live in such crammed one-room houses. He was most disturbed by the peculiar reason behind the Batwa people's singing and dancing before bed. They often would end the day hungry and had figured that they could dance themselves into a fatigue that enabled them to sleep on empty stomachs. That pattern was repeated until they found food.

When you hear Claude talk about his decision to help the Batwa in his native Burundi, you hear the heart of a man who acknowledged the mountainous proportion of the fathering task but did not cower. He determined in his heart to make a difference in their lives. He worked with others to write one of Africa's best untold stories. This Batwa community now owns land, respectable housing, an abundance of food, thriving economic ventures and the respect of their neighbors[21]. That is the kind of transformation that ordinary men like Claude can cause when they determine to father.

There is a Claude in every man that chooses to father. The benefits are better than any treasure. Nations and generations await your decision to step up to the fathering role that was hardwired into every man by God the Father.

Determine to show up for the responsibilities that come with fathering. Determine today to stand up and be counted as a father. Determine to take the fatherless under your wing. The fatherless may be young boys and girls. They may be broken grown men and women with seemingly okay lives and eight-to-five jobs. The fatherless may even be communities around you or an entire nation. If the fatherlessness of an individual or a community has tagged at your heart strings, determine to father them. Determine to love them, cherish them and cheer them on. Every human being on earth desires to be fueled by the love and steady hand of a father as they sojourn through life.

Your fathering will flourish. It will flourish in the city and in the country, in your home and your community. Your children shall consider themselves blessed because of you. They shall walk the path of life with a confidence that comes from those that have been fathered. Your name will be mentioned by your children among the many great fathers that have walked the surface of the earth. Your name shall be used by your descendants with pleasant memories. The impact and influence of your fathering will span ten generations and more.

May the Lord bless you and take care of you. May the Lord be kind and gracious to you. May the Lord look on you with favor and give you peace. Amen.

It is my passion to see fathers have a much easier job fathering their children than our forefathers did. I would like to continue walking this journey with you. Kindly let me know how helpful this book has been to you. If you are keen on working with tools that can help you be a better father, we have GOLD IN FATHERING Intensive Seminars and Workshops that can be run in any city in the world. Drop me an email at *chrismugga@ gmail.com* and let's chat about your involvement.

End Notes

1. *U.S. Census Bureau, Current Population Survey, "Living Arrangements of Children under 18 Years/1 and Marital Status of Parents by Age, Sex, Race, and Hispanic Origin/2 and Selected Characteristics of the Child for all Children 2010." Table C3. Internet Release Date November, 2010. (First citation by National Center for Fathering)*

2. *National Centre for Fathering, 'The Extent of Fatherlessness'. Available from: <http://www.fathers.com/ statistics-and-research/the-extent-of-fatherlessness/>. [19 October, 2015].*

3. *National Center for Fathering, Fathering in America Poll, January, 1999. (First citation from National Center for Fathering). [19 October 2015].*

4. *Henry, M 2013, 'The cost of Absent Fathers', The Gleaner, 26 May. Available from: http://jamaica-gleaner.com/ gleaner/20130526/focus/focus3.html. [21 October 2015].*

5. *The World Bank, Female headed households Data. Available from: <http://data.worldbank.org/indicator/SP.HOU. FEMA.ZS>. [21 October 2015].*

6. *National Centre for Fathering, The Extent of Fatherlessness. Available from: <http://www.fathers.com/ statistics-and-research/the-extent-of-fatherlessness/>. [19 October, 2015].*

7. *Atisco Entertainment News September 2015, Atiscoblog. 27 September 2015. Atisco Entertainment: Blog. Available from: < http://www.atiscoblog.com/2015/09/chris-brown-says-hes-tired-of.html>. [28 September 2015].*

8. *The Try Guys Try labor Pain Simulation. Motherhoood: Part 4, 2015 (video file), Available from: https://www.youtube. com/watch?v=b81Cr97ANrk>. [28 October 2015].*

10. *Breen, M & Cockram, S 2011, Building A Discipling Culture, second edition, 3dm, Pawleys Island.*

12. *Schroer WJ., 'Generations X, Y, Z and the others', The Social Librarian, Available from: <http://www.socialmarketing. org/newsletter/features/generation1.htm>. [14 October 2015].*

13. *Schmidt SM, 2014. 'F.B.I confirms a sharp rise in mass shootings since 2000', NewYork Times, 25 September. Available from: <http://www.nytimes.com/2014/09/25/us/25shooters. html?_r=0> [15 October 2015].*

14. Barnes, A, 'Exodus 2, Barnes Notes', Available from: <http://Biblehub.com/commentaries/barnes/exodus/2.htm>. [14 October 2015].

15. Rodeheaver, S 2011. 'Exodus 4:18-31 God seeks Moses' life', The Voice, 8 November. Available from:<http://www. crivoice.org/Biblestudy/exodus/bbex7.html>. [5 October 2015].

16. Cambridge Bible for Schools and Colleges & Ellicott's Commentary for English readers. 'Exodus 1:8'. Available from: <http://Biblehub.com/commentaries/exodus/1-8.htm>. [14 October 2015].

17. The Hesitant Prize Fighter August 2010, The Hesitant Prize Fighter: Blog. Available from: <https://tben.wordpress. com/2010/08/21/the-timeline-of-the-lives-of-isaac-jacob-and-joseph/>. [14 October, 2015].

18. Nikondeha, C, Amahoro Conversations moves to Mozambique, 2010. Available from: < http://www.amahoro-africa.org/amahoro_africa/2010/10/amahoro-conversations-moves-to-mozambique.html> [21 October 2015].

19. Kazoza Finance 2015,Social networking group, (Face Book), 23 October. Available from: < https://www.facebook. com/Kazoza-Finance-595808953809251/>. [23 October 2015]

20. Communities of Hope 2015, Batwa of Burundi. Available from: <http://www.communitiesofhope.tv/news/category/ batwa-of-burundi/>. [28 October 2015].

21. Irakoze, YD 2014, 'Batwa salute Communities of Hope Support', Iwacu English News 26 June. Available from: < http://www.iwacu-burundi.org/blogs/english/batwa-salute-communities-of-hope-support/>. [22 October 2015].